INTENTION, SINCERITY AND TRUTHFULNESS

Kitāb al-niyya wa'l-ikhlāṣ wa'l-ṣidq

BOOK XXXVII of
THE REVIVAL OF THE RELIGIOUS SCIENCES
Iḥyā' ʿulūm al-dīn

OTHER TITLES IN THE ISLAMIC TEXTS SOCIETY
AL-GHAZĀLĪ SERIES

FROM *The Revival of the Religious Sciences*

Al-Ghazālī on Invocations & Supplications

Al-Ghazālī on the Manners Relating to Eating

Al-Ghazālī on the Lawful & the Unlawful

Al-Ghazālī on Conduct in Travel

Al-Ghazālī on Disciplining the Soul & Breaking the Two Desires

Al-Ghazālī on the Condemnation of Pride & Self-Admiration

Al-Ghazālī on Patience & Thankfulness

Al-Ghazālī on Poverty & Abstinence

Al-Ghazālī on Love, Longing, Intimacy & Contentment

Al-Ghazālī on Vigilance & Self-examination

Al-Ghazālī on the Remembrance of Death & the Afterlife

OTHER WORKS

Al-Ghazālī on the Ninety-Nine Beautiful Names of God
(*al-Maqṣad al-asnā fī sharḥ asmā' Allāh al-ḥusnā*)

Al-Ghazālī Letter to a Disciple
(*Ayyuhā'l-walad*)

AL-GHAZĀLĪ ON INTENTION SINCERITY AND TRUTHFULNESS

Kitāb al-niyya wa'l-ikhlāṣ wa'l-ṣidq ·

BOOK XXXVII of THE REVIVAL OF THE RELIGIOUS SCIENCES

Iḥyā' ʿulūm al-dīn · translated with INTRODUCTION and Notes by ANTHONY F. SHAKER

2nd Ed. with al-Ghazālī's Introduction to the *Revival of the Religious Sciences* ·

First edition published 2013 by The Islamic Texts Society

This second edition published 2016 by
The Islamic Texts Society
Miller's House
Kings Mill Lane
Great Shelford
Cambridge CB22 5EN, U.K.

Reprinted 2019, 2023, 2024

British Library Cataloguing-in-Publication Data.
A catalogue record for this book is
available from the British Library.

ISBN: 978 1911141 341 paper

CONTENTS

Al-Ghazālī's Introduction to the
Revival of the Religious Sciences IX

Introduction XIX

THE BOOK OF INTENTION, SINCERITY AND TRUTHFULNESS

[Prologue 1]

PART I: ON INTENTION

CHAPTER ONE: An Exposition of the Merit of Intention 5

CHAPTER TWO: An Exposition of the Reality of Intention 11

CHAPTER THREE: An Exposition of the Inner Meaning of the Prophet's Words: 'The intention of the believer is better than his deed' 17

CHAPTER FOUR: A Classification of How Actions are Related to Intention 24

CHAPTER FIVE: An Exposition on that Intention is Not a Matter of Choice 37

PART II: ON SINCERITY, ITS MERIT, REALITY AND DEGREES

CHAPTER SIX: An Exposition of the Merit of Sincerity 49

CHAPTER SEVEN: An Exposition of the Reality of Sincerity 57

CHAPTER EIGHT: An Exposition of What the Great Masters have Said About Sincerity 64

CHAPTER NINE: An Exposition of the Levels of Blemishes and Flaws that Cloud Sincerity 68

CHAPTER TEN: An Exposition on the Judgement of the Tarnished Act and the Worthiness of the Reward for it 72

PART III: ON TRUTHFULNESS, ITS MERIT AND REALITY

CHAPTER ELEVEN: An Exposition of the Merit of Truthfulness 81

CHAPTER TWELVE: An Exposition of the Reality of Truthfulness, Its Meaning and Levels 85

Notes 99
Appendix: Persons Cited in Text 109
Bibliography 119
Index to Qur'ānic Quotations 123
General Index 125

For Nicolas and Nadim, my nephews,
and our unforgettable table conversations on life
and on mystics returning from the summit for the whole truth!
Souvenons-nous!

Al-Ghazālī's Introduction to the *Revival of the Religious Sciences*

The importance of Imam Ghazālī's Introduction to the Revival of the Religious Sciences *cannot be overstated; it outlines the reasons and motives for the writing of the* Revival *and it explains the structure of the work as a whole. The Islamic Texts Society has decided to include this Introduction at the beginning of all its translations from the* Revival, *including in revised editions of earlier translations. In the list of the forty chapters below, the choice of translation for the titles of the not-yet-published chapters is not restrictive; the final translations will be left to the individual translators and the list below will be periodically updated with the latest chapter headings.*

In the Name of God, the Compassionate, the Merciful

FIRSTLY, I PRAISE GOD with many continuous praises; though the praise of those who praise is meagre in front of what is due to His majesty.

Secondly, I invoke blessings and peace upon His Messenger—blessings that encompass along with the leader of mankind (*sayyid al-bashar*)[A] all other prophets.

Thirdly, I ask for His guidance (Gloried and Exalted is He) as I resolve to write a book for the revival of the religious sciences.

Fourthly, I hasten to put a stop to your censure O critic who—among those who reject [what we say]—has gone to extremes in his criticism, and who—among those who deny [us] and are heedless—is immoderate in his chiding and rejection.[B]

[A] The Prophet Muḥammad.

[B] It is not clear if Ghazālī had a particular person in mind when he penned

My tongue has been set loose, and the responsibility to speak out and to discourse have become incumbent on me due to your persistent blindness to the obvious truth, your obstinacy in backing falsehood and in embellishing ignorance, and your stirring up hostility against him who has given preference to stepping somewhat aside from social conventions and who has verged slightly from formality. [He does this] for the sake of acting according to the dictates of knowledge and in eagerness to gain what God (Great and Glorious is He) has commanded in purifying the soul and rectifying the heart, thus somewhat redeeming a life wasted and in the hope of escaping complete rack and ruin. Hence, he seeks to avoid the risk of being associated with those about whom the Law giver (may God bless him and grant him peace) has said, 'The one who will be most severely punished on the Day of Judgement is he who was granted knowledge (*ʿālim*)[A] and whom God (glory be to Him) did not make benefit from his knowledge.'[B]

By my life, there is no reason for the persistence of your opposition except for the malady that has encompassed the vast majority—indeed the multitudes. [The malady of] the inability to discern the weight of the matter, the ignorance of how grave the situation is and how crucial the issue, that the Hereafter is approaching and that this life is departing, that the end of life is near and the journey still far, that the provision is scanty and the danger immense, that the way is blocked, that for the discerning critic the knowledge and the acts that are purely for God are what avail, and that to pursue the path of the Hereafter—with all its many dangers and without a guide or companion—is exhausting and arduous.

this very severe and direct criticism here and below. Its personal nature does suggest that he did have someone in mind, but he could equally have used this form as a general accusation against a specific group.

[A] The term *ʿālim* (pl. *ʿulamāʾ*) has been translated both as 'he who has been granted or who possesses knowledge' and as 'scholar' according to the context.

[B] Ṭabarānī, *al-Muʿjam al-ṣaghīr*, I.182.

The guides of the way are those who possess knowledge (*ʿulamāʾ*) who are the heirs of the prophets.[A] This age is devoid of them and those who remain are impersonators; most have been overpowered by the devil and been led astray by iniquity. Each one is engrossed with his earthly gain; he sees what is right objectionable and what is objectionable right; thus the banner of religion has been pulled down and the beacon of guidance all over the world is extinguished.

[These impersonators] deceive people into thinking that knowledge is only decrees of the state (*fatāwā ḥukūma*) that judges use in order to resolve disputes when there is disturbance by the rabble, or a form of debating which a person seeking to show off equips himself with in order to gain superiority and the upper hand, or ornate language which a preacher uses to lure in the common people. These three [means] are all they could find to snare illegal gain and to net the vanities [of the world].

Now the knowledge of the path to the Hereafter (*ʿilm ṭarīq al-ākhira*)—which was followed by the pious predecessors and which was called by God (Glorified is He) in His Book: law (*fiqh*), wisdom (*ḥikma*), knowledge (*ʿilm*), luminescence (*ḍiyāʾ*), light (*nūr*), guidance (*hidāya*), right-direction (*rushd*)—has become among people a thing hidden and forgotten.

As this [situation] is a calamitous fissure in religion and as the times are dark, I concluded that it is crucial to undertake the composition of this book in order to revive the religious sciences, to seek out the methods of the previous leaders [of religion], and to clarify what the prophets and the pious predecessors considered beneficial knowledge (may God grant them all peace).

I divided it into four quarters: the Quarter of the Acts of Worship (*rubʿ al-ʿibādāt*), the Quarter of the Norms of Daily Life (*rubʿ al-ʿādāt*), the Quarter of the Moral Vices (*rubʿ al-muhlikāt*) and the Quarter of the Saving Virtues (*rubʿ al-munjiyāt*).

[A] ʿIrāqī, 1.6 says this is in Abū Dāʾūd, Tirmidhī, Ibn Māja and in *Ṣaḥīḥ* Ibn Ḥibbān on the authority of Abū al-Dardāʾ.

I began the whole [of the work] with 'The Book of Knowledge'[A] (*Kitāb al-ʿilm*) because [knowledge] is of the utmost importance. Firstly, I reveal the knowledge that God (Great and Glorious is He) ordered the elite (*aʿyān*) to seek in the words of His Prophet (may God bless him and grant him peace) when he said, 'Seeking knowledge is a legal obligation (*farīḍa*) for every Muslim';[B] then, I differentiate [in the book] between knowledge that is beneficial and [knowledge] that is harmful, for may God bless him and grant him peace said, 'We seek refuge in You from knowledge that does not benefit';[C] and I illustrate how far the people of this age have departed from right conduct, and how deceived they are by glossy illusions[D] and by their contentment with the husk rather than the kernel of knowledge.

The Quarter of the Acts of Worship is made up of ten Books:

1 The Book of Knowledge
2 The Book of the Foundations of the Articles of Faith
3 The Book of the Mysteries of Purity
4 The Book of the Mysteries of the Prayer
5 The Book of the Mysteries of Almsgiving
6 The Book of the Mysteries of Fasting
7 The Book of the Mysteries of the Pilgrimage
8 The Book of Ways of Reciting of the Qur'ān
9 The Book of Invocations and Supplications
10 The Book of Classification of Litanies and the Division of the Night Vigil

The Quarter of the Norms of Daily Life is made up of ten Books:

11 The Book of the Manners Related to Eating
12 The Book of Conduct in Marriage
13 The Book of Ways of Earning and Making a Living

A We have retained Book for the titles of the chapters of the *Revival*.

B Ibn Mājā 224.

C Muslim 2722.

D Lit. 'mirage' (*sarāb*).

14 The Book of the Lawful and the Unlawful
15 The Book of Ways of Friendship, Brotherhood and Companionship
16 The Book of Conduct in Seclusion
17 The Book of Conduct in Travel
18 The Book of Conduct in Audition and Ecstasy
19 The Book of Enjoining the Good and Prohibiting Evil
20 The Book of Conduct of Living and the Qualities of Prophethood

The Quarter of the Moral Vices is made up of ten Books:

21 The Book of Expounding the Wonders of the Heart
22 The Book of Disciplining the Soul
23 The Book of Breaking the Two Desires
24 The Book of the Vices of the Tongue
25 The Book of Condemnation of Anger, Rancour and Envy
26 The Book of Condemnation of the World
27 The Book of Condemnation of Avarice and Love of Wealth
28 The Book of Condemnation of Status and Ostentation
29 The Book of Condemnation of Pride and Conceit
30 The Book of Condemnation of Self-delusion

The Quarter of the Saving Virtues is made up of ten Books:

31 The Book of Repentance
32 The Book of Patience and Thankfulness
33 The Book of Fear and Hope
34 The Book of Poverty and Abstinence
35 The Book of Unity of God and Reliance upon Him
36 The Book of Love, Longing, Intimacy and Contentment
37 The Book of Intention, Sincerity and Truthfulness
38 The Book of Vigilance and Self-examination
39 The Book of Reflection
40 The Book of the Remembrance of Death and the Afterlife

As to the Quarter of the Acts of Worship, I mention in it the mysteries of their conduct, the subtleties of their ways, the secrets of their meanings, and what the practicing scholar (*al-ʿālim al-ʿāmil*) cannot do without; he would not be among the scholars of the Hereafter if he were not versed in these. Much of this has been neglected in the studies of jurisprudence.

In the Quarter of the Norms of Daily Life, I discuss the secrets of the [various] relations that take place between people (*muʿāmalāt*),[A] their deeper meanings, the subtleties of their ways, and the mysteries of the piety (*waraʿ*) that should run through them. [All] these are what no religious person (*mutadayyin*) can do without.

In the Quarter of the Moral Vices, I list every reprehensible character trait (*khuluq madhmūm*) that the Qur'ān commanded to be uprooted, and the soul to be cleansed and the heart to be purified thereof. I include for each of these character traits its definition (*ḥadd*) and its reality (*ḥaqīqa*), then the cause from which it derives, the evils that result from it, the signs by which it can be recognised, and the different remedies that can be used to eliminate it.

Accompanying all this are proofs from Qur'ānic verses, Prophetic reports (*akhbār*) and narratives (*āthār*).

As to the Quarter of the Saving Virtues, I mention every laudable character trait and every desirable quality of those near [to God] (*muqarrabūn*) and of the righteous (*ṣiddīqūn*) through which the servant can gain proximity to the Lord of the worlds. For every quality I give its definition and its reality, the means by which it can be attained, the fruits that are derived from it, the signs by which it can be recognised, the merits which make it desirable, and the ways that it has been affirmed by the Law (*sharʿ*) and by the intellect (*ʿaql*).

[A] The plural *muʿāmalāt* (sing. *muʿāmala*) does not have the same meaning as *ʿilm al-muʿāmala* below and therefore they have been translated differently according to Ghazālī's intention for each.

Other titles have been written about some of these topics,[A] but this [present] work is distinguished from them in five ways:

Firstly, it clarifies what is complicated in them and elucidates what they have mentioned in passing.

Secondly, it organises what is scattered in them and systematises what is disparate in them.

Thirdly, it summarises what they have overly discussed and gives precision to what they have affirmed.

Fourthly, it deletes what they have repeated and corroborates what they have formulated.

Fifthly, it clarifies ambiguous matters that are difficult to understand and that have never even been the subject of books. For though all [who write] may follow a single method, this does not preclude each one who pursues [this method] from paying special attention to a matter that concerns him and which his colleagues may not know about, or may be aware of it but overlooked it in writing, or may not have overlooked it but something caused them to turn away from it.

While it includes all the [above mentioned] sciences, these are the [five] specific attributes of this work.

Two things prompted me to compose this book in four quarters. The first and primary motive is that this arrangement is indispensable when researching and elaborating [on a subject], given that the knowledge by which we approach the Hereafter is divided into 'the knowledge of contingent actions' (*ᶜilm al-muᶜāmala*)[B] and 'direct knowledge' (*ᶜilm al-mukāshafa*).[C]

[A] In writing the *Revival*, Ghazālī was fully aware of the religious literature of his time and, in the *Revival*, he both draws on a number of titles (for example, Makkī's *Qūt al-qulūb*) and takes this literature a step further.

[B] *Muᶜāmala* (pl. *muᶜāmalāt*) is usually translated as 'transaction', 'procedure', 'treatment'. But for Ghazālī, there is a return to the root of the term in *ᶜamala*, 'to act'. In translating *ᶜilm al-muᶜāmala* as 'the knowledge of contingent actions', we have taken both Ghazālī's own definition and the root of the term into consideration.

[C] In Sufism, *mukāshafa* is a technical term meaning 'unveiling' and 'direct

By direct knowledge, I mean [the knowledge] whose only requirement is to reveal the object of knowledge (*maʿlūm*) and nothing else.

By the knowledge of contingent actions, I mean [the knowledge] of the actions that necessarily accompany direct knowledge.[A]

The aim of this book is exclusively the knowledge of contingent actions and not direct knowledge which—despite it being the goal of those who seek and the aspiration for the vision of the righteous—is beyond being documented in books. The knowledge of contingent actions is a means to it. The prophets (may God bless them and grant them peace) only spoke to people about the knowledge of the path (*ʿilm al-ṭarīq*) and about guidance to it. As to direct knowledge, they only mentioned it through symbol and allusion, and by way of comparison and in a general fashion, knowing that people's understanding falls short of comprehending it. Now, those who possess knowledge are the heirs of the prophets and thus they cannot verge from the method of emulating and imitating [the prophets].

Knowledge of contingent actions is divided into outer knowledge (*ʿilm ẓāhir*), by which I mean the knowledge of the actions for bodily parts; and inner knowledge (*ʿilm bāṭin*), by which I mean the knowledge of the actions of the heart.

or experiential knowledge'; it is linked with *dhawq* 'tasting'. The term has been translated as 'revelation' (Nabih Amin Faris, *The Book of Knowledge*, p. XIV), but it is clear from Ghazālī's definition that it is not revelation as *waḥy*, but is direct spiritual knowledge of immutable truths.

[A] It should not be understood from this very concise definition that Ghazālī intends each individual to act exclusively on his or her own direct knowledge. The actions referred to here are those derived from the Qur'ān, the *Sunna* of the Prophet, and the example of the pious predecessors and the saints; thus actions based in revelation and in the direct knowledge of the Prophet and the saintly. Each of the chapters of the *Revival* invariably starts with reference to Qur'anic verses, the traditions of the Prophet and the narratives of the Companions and the saints, making them the example to be followed.

What applies to the bodily parts is either worship (*ʿibāda*) or norms of daily life (*ʿāda*).[A]

What occurs in the heart—which by dint of being veiled from the senses is part of the heavenly realm (*malakūt*)—is either commendable (*maḥmūd*) or reprehensible (*madhmūm*).[B]

Thus, this knowledge [of contingent actions] by necessity divides into two halves: outer and inner. The outer half, which is connected to the bodily parts, is itself divided into worship and norms of daily life; while the inner half, which is connected to the states of the heart and the attributes of the soul, is divided into either what is reprehensible or what is commendable. Therefore, the result is four parts and no examination of the knowledge of contingent actions can go beyond these divisions.

The secondary motive [for composing this book]: I have found that—[despite jurisprudence] being exploited by those who do not fear God to boast, and their making use of its prestige and standing in competing [with each other]—there is a genuine desire for knowledge on behalf of the students of jurisprudence. [Thus, in imitation of the works of jurisprudence,] it is divided into four quarters; for he who takes on the garb of the beloved becomes beloved. I believe that styling the book in the form of [books of] jurisprudence will gently lead hearts [to it]. This was the reason why one of those who wanted to draw the attention of persons in authority to [the science of] medicine structured it in the form of an astrological almanac, arranged it into tables and numbers, and called it 'The Almanac of Health', that their familiarity with this kind [of science] may draw them to reading [his title].

Gently leading hearts to the knowledge that benefits everlasting life is more important than leading them to medicine that

[A] Elaborated in the Quarter of Acts of Worship and the Quarter of Norms of Daily Life.

[B] Elaborated in the Quarter of the Moral Vices and the Quarter of the Saving Virtues.

only benefits the health of the body. The fruit of this knowledge is the health of hearts and souls and the arrival through it to life that never ends. How can the medicine that is used to heal bodies, necessarily destined before long to corruption, compare with this!

We ask God (glory be to Him) guidance to what is right and just, for He is the Generous, the Munificent.

The Islamic Texts Society
Rabīᶜ al-thanī 1436/February 2015

INTRODUCTION

A PIVOTAL THINKER, Abū Ḥāmid Muḥammad b. Muḥammad b. Muḥammad b. Aḥmad al-Ghazālī (d. 1111) studied under no less a figure than the Imām al-Ḥaramayn, a position occupied at the time by celebrated Shāfiʿī jurist and *mutakallim* Abū al-Maʿālī al-Juwaynī (d. 1085). Not only did Juwaynī help shape his student's intellect, perhaps inspiring or triggering his self-confessed spiritual transformation later in life; he also epitomised the growing symbiosis between two mainstream approaches to questions of broadly devotional and philosophical import: on the one hand, a dialectical theology (*kalām*) hewed partly to Ibn Ḥanbal's dogged and biting criticisms of the Ashʿarites' overwrought theories, and on the other, Sufism. By the time Niẓām al-Mulk (d. 1092)—the Seljuk Sultan's vizier—entered office, the teachings of the most revered early mystics had been faithfully recorded and propagated throughout the known (Islamic) world. Of the two, only Sufism—finding legitimacy—'survived' into modern times, albeit in newfangled, often socially isolated forms that bear little resemblance to its rich past.

Another clear representative of this symbiosis was Abū al-Qāsim al-Qushayrī (d. 1074). He was instrumental in gaining Sufi discourse new acceptance under the expanding political order of the Seljuk dynasty. Many of the sayings and key definitions in the *Book of Intention, Sincerity and Truthfulness* are traceable to Qushayrī's famous treatise, *al-Risāla fī ʿilm al-taṣawwuf*. However, Ghazālī borrowed mainly from Abū Ṭālib al-Makkī's *Qūt al-qulūb*, a valued source on the teachings of the early mystics and ascetics. Far more systematic than Makkī (d. 996), however, he adapted the themes found in Makkī's book to his *magnum opus*, expatiating on subjects ranging from fasting and prayer to intention and knowledge.

A direct beneficiary of this new socio-intellectual dynamic, which also included thinkers like Bayhaqī (d. 1066), Ghazālī articulated his insights into the most divisive legal and philosophical issues of his day in numerous works. Hardly surprising, then, given such breadth of mind, that he should take stock of the 'religious sciences' (*ʿulūm al-dīn*) as a whole. The fruits of his labour came in a long but accessible work widely known as *Iḥyā' ʿulūm al-dīn* (The Revival of the Religious Sciences), his *magnum opus*, of which the present is the thirty-seventh chapter. Ghazālī hoped with this monumental work to give definitive shape to the 'sciences of religion'.

The Study of 'Religion' in the Spirit of Ghazālī

It would be a mistake to regard 'religious' in our rendering of '*dīn*' in *Iḥyā' ʿulūm al-dīn* as synonymous with 'ritual', 'dogma' or the idle speculations of some mystery cult *à la romaine*. Ghazālī, like the overwhelming majority of medieval Islam's thinkers, regarded the 'sciences of religion' as a *practical* pursuit, of which the word *muʿāmala* provides an accurate indication. To be sure, these sciences (*ʿulūm*) inquired into issues of great consequence to every religious devotee. But the word *ʿilm* (science), one easily forgets, properly refers to a *method* of approach to an 'object of inquiry' which a community of minds happens to recognize, rather than merely a set of beliefs, rituals, etc. While not exactly rigorous in the manner of philosophy or physics (with its own potential for metaphysical extrapolation), *ʿulūm al-dīn* nevertheless purported to cover the entire spectrum of human activity, in keeping with God's repeated injunctions. The Qur'ān addresses man as a single entity and as a multitude, as an individual and as a community, and it speaks of past and present, Muslim and non-Muslim, etc. Fundamentally, Ghazālī had only to reaffirm this quintessentially *Qur'ānic* vision of 'devotional' life writ large.

This is not to say that the comprehensive view of religious practice he came to adopt collapsed all epistemological distinctions into a single dimension that modern fundamentalists today might triumphally name 'religious'.

On the one hand, Ghazālī instead designated the pure and immediate knowledge obtained of any object of intellectual contemplation whatsoever as the province of *ʿilm al-mukāshafa*. Based on that knowledge, on the other, but joined to action was a knowledge he associated with *ʿilm al-mu ʿāmala*.[A] Religion (*dīn*), in this latter sense, entailed a practical orientation anchored simply to the seeker's obligation to establish a direct, personal relationship with God, and at the very least with the aid of the cognitive faculties with which he or she was endowed. This, rather than the narrow preoccupations of modern-day 'religion', encompassed every aspect of human life, but based on pre-given elements not unlike the premises of a logical syllogism, which elements may comprise the contents of sense perception no less than the articles of faith. By themselves, nevertheless, the limited faculties offered only a truncated view of the 'realities of things' (*ḥaqāʾiq al-ashyāʾ*), though beyond them God's succour continued in myriad forms.

Ghazālī further divided this knowledge into the science of external conduct (where the acts of worship were performed through the external organs of the body) and the science of the interior (which dealt with the functions of the 'heart' and the inner senses).[B] Under this second aspect, the science of *practical* religion was, in his view, virtually indistinguishable from the 'science of the heart's states', or *ʿilm aḥwāl al-qalb*.

At the same time, the religious sciences remained distinct from the profane disciplines, whether philosophical or practical. The domain of philosophy consisted of logic, metaphysics, physics, mathematics, etc. Ghazālī deemed some theoretical sciences useful, others less so or downright harmful.[C] It must be remembered that he was a trenchant critic not only of the *falāsifa*, who

[A] Ghazālī, 'The Book of Knowledge', *Iḥyāʾ ʿulūm al-dīn* 3-4.

[B] *Ibid.*, 4

[C] *Ibid.*, 2.

espoused the earliest, Peripatetic form of philosophy under the aegis of Islam and were largely responsible for reworking the taxonomic and epistemological scheme for the profane sciences.[A] He also laced into a brand of Ismāʿīlism propagating an arcane doctrine of knowledge that was heavily dependent on Neo-Platonism. These Hellenised schools of thought explored many of the same questions that *kalām* did, but the abstract modes of reasoning employed by both camps had precedents predating even Islam and often cleaved them to the ponderous logic of the ancients. No matter how closely the proponents of short-lived currents like *kalām* claimed to stick to the core issues of religion, the tools of logic stood at a great remove from the Divine Word which the *Sunna* of the Prophet Muḥammad brought to life. Even when pressed into the service of religion, and even where its logical premises were plainly on the order of beliefs, opinions or articles of faith, the art of logic seemed a distant shadow of the faith familiar to Muslims, however reformed or creatively adapted to new needs. Logic, it was occasionally argued, must therefore be derived from a foreign tongue, Greek; whereas faith was rooted in the concrete language of revelation, Arabic.

In consequence, the ethereal heights to which philosophers appeared to confine their reasoning hardly endeared them to the Qur'ān exegetes and the jurists, especially, some of who simply judged the views of the *falāsifa* anathema to the religious spirit. Therefore, the whole enterprise of *falsafa* was called into question and, as an independent school of thought, nipped in the bud.[B]

[A] The *falāsifa* inherited and strenuously studied the main works of ancient Greece and their Hellenic commentators; most prominent among the *falāsifa* were Fārābī and Ibn Sīnā.

[B] The word *falsafa*, derived from the Greek, continued to be used into modern times, especially in Iran, but as a distinct intellectual current it became defunct. The fate of *falsafa* as a separate method of philosophical and scientific investigation, however, says nothing about the subsequent flowering of systematic science up to at least the eighteenth century, a development without parallel in the annals of history. In fact, this is precisely the *long* period that

But this by no means implied that subsequent thinking had automatically to ignore either its logical or extra-logical (i.e., 'metaphysical') achievements. It did not. Logic is a tool and was so considered. Thinking may move beyond its narrow rules and jurisdiction but not expunge it, any more than quantum physics expunged Newtonian physics.

In the present book, Ghazālī's cogitations on life's paradoxes come alive with quotations and anecdotes culled about the Companions of the Prophet, the generation that followed, and the earliest ascetics of Islam—effectively leaving the experts and the doctors of law out of the *Iḥyā'*. But the philosophical undertones and rigour of his vulgarizing works in general are hard to miss. In the *Mizān al-ʿamal* (The Balance of Action)—an important ethical work permeated with insights into the profundities of the human act and powers—Ghazālī insisted that what was religio-legal and what was rational science complemented rather than contradicted each other.[A] In hindsight, this seems like an understatement, because his entire thinking is driven by a deeper layer of *philosophical* understanding, not to be confused with the *speculative* mien he associated with many of his adversaries. It is good to keep this in mind when reading Ghazālī.

That said, Ghazālī was neither a philosopher nor a dialectical theologian in the strict sense. As a thinker, he was given sometimes to surprisingly radical thinking on the intricacies of reasoning and epistemology, especially later in life. In this sense, he does not fit the common definition of the '*mutakallim*', lucidly formulated by Sharīf Jurjānī, as someone in pursuit of 'the investigative science of the creeds of Islam.'[B] In any case, *kalām* paled before the sophistication of *falsafa* or even the 'philosophical theology' of a Thomas Aquinas. Neither Ghazālī nor, for that matter, the

Western academics have taken to calling anonymously 'post-Ghazālī', even though it constituted the main drama.

[A] Ghazālī, *Mizān al-ʿAmal* 146.

[B] *Ibid.*, 146.

mutakallimūn themselves argued for a full-fledged *theology* in the quasi-philosophical manner of Latin Scholasticism. Latin Europe knew Ghazālī chiefly through his *Tahāfut al-falāsifa* (Refutation of the Philosophers), which up to a point, helped inure Christian theology against the 'pagan' doctrines of the Greeks. Still, his critique of Ibn Sīnā (*Lat.*, Avicenna) was too sweeping to benefit the *mutakallimūn* or to leave *kalām* much room to grow into a 'queen of the sciences'. Whatever the *Tahāfut* may have signalled to Latin Europe, he never meant to take his critique to the *theological* heights of the Schoolmen, since he considered *kalām* too thin to bear the weight of a self-complete science. Despite his dim view of the over-rationalising *mutakallimūn*, *kalām*'s links to Hellenic doctrines were nevertheless more tenuous than those of *falsafa*, not to say ably camouflaged by its authors. Although this made that branch of learning more defensible than *falsafa* in the eyes of the nascent orthodoxy, he confessed having read and written in this field without ever finding satisfaction.[A] *Kalām*, he declared, was well adapted to its ends, but not to his. In declaring this, he meant neither to deny the utility of dialectical theology within its own precinct, nor to stir unwarranted interest in it, presumably for fear it might mislead the untrained to be remiss in practical life. This pragmatic appraisal was pretty standard; it remained so for Ṣadr al-Dīn Qūnawī (d. 1274), Ibn ʿArabī's most brilliant and influential student, and henceforth for nearly every mystic-philosopher who had no intrinsic reason to tolerate the ruminated excesses of the *mutakallimūn*.

But if Ghazālī was neither a philosopher nor a theologian in the strict sense, what was he? This is a hard question, one more easily answered by reference to the broader intellectual synthesis inquiries taking shape in his day.

[A] Ghazālī, *al-Munqidh min al-ḍalāl* 16.

The Problem of Living Human Agency

Simply put, alone the dialectical theologians appeared incapable of establishing what Ghazālī—in the spirit of the great mystics, not to mention the Ismāʿīlīs themselves—called the '*mizān*' (balance), a balance or algorithm of practical living. In fact, every independent science needed a *mizān*. But instead of the mental acrobatics of the *mutakallimūn* over free choice and moral responsibility, so dear to the Muʿtazila, his gaze fell upon 'experience' (*dhawq*, or lit., tasting), which inevitably gave human agency as well as receptivity pride of place. In this respect, the Sufis, whom he esteemed, were clearly of a different order than the *mutakallimūn*. Whereas the latter defended the faith by rationalising about justice and the human act, the Sufis took the *experience* that lay at the core of the human act as their prime focus. Far from passive, experience as a process (not just a reception of information) was integral to Ghazālī's concept of the human act and initiative and the religious sciences generally.

This perspective obviously drew him closer to the Sufis, for whom the path to salvation was inconceivable without the *experience* of continual, purposeful action, and for whom cognisance (*maʿrifa*) and practice were joined at the root[A]—in the bosom of life, one might say.

In order to render this curious embryonic origin in layman's terms, Ghazālī laboured to keep the technical tone of even his finer arguments and definitions to a minimum across the thematic divisions of the *Iḥyā'*. Overall, one pictures a learned, well-rounded scholar-teacher seeking—at least within the rough guidelines furnished by his spiritual autobiography[B]—to balance the exterior and the interior of man's existential dynamics through the liberating force of learning, which was both a practice and an act of worship.

[A] *Ibid.*, 35.

[B] Cf. Ghazālī, *al-Munqidh min al-ḍalāl*.

But the *Iḥyā'* is not an ethical work, any more than it is a work exclusively concerned with acts of worship. This is true even where he urges his coreligionists to look after every aspect of worship in order to *render service to Islam*. Its main teaching, arguably, is that every human being of sound mind can (not just ought to) reflect on 'what is beyond material things' in every sphere of activity so as to point him- or herself to the Hereafter. Sound knowledge engenders sound action, which in turn deepens knowledge of both the material world and what transcends it. Ultimately, that knowledge which man possesses could only be of God, in contradistinction to 'what is other than God'. But it remains that for Ghazālī only concrete action, born of the noetic consciousness of the individual's relationship with God and His attributes, determined the reward of the Hereafter.

In this 'practical' scheme, the centrality of experience—inconceivable without individual perception powers or a *psyche*—need not tint Ghazālī's pronouncements with modern-type psychologism. This is an issue well worth examining, as it may help us determine more precisely how Islam's learning tradition and sciences developed in the centuries that followed.

The Act of Worship

Kalābādhī (d. 990), who codified Sufism's key expressions, invoked Muḥammad b. Sinjān's terse view of piety as the rejection of 'what is other than God'. Piety signified to Ghazālī 'the exclusion of what is other than God from one's purview.'[A] This, he wrote, was true sincerity. On this subject he wrote,

> The habitual activities of someone dominated by the love of God and the Hereafter acquire the attribute of his preoccupation, becoming sincerity. The activities of someone whose soul is dominated by this world, by grandeur and by

[A] Kalābādhī, *al-Taʿarruf li-madhhab ahl al-tasawwuf* 116.

> supremacy—in short, 'everything other than God'—acquire just this attribute [i.e., the attribute of 'worshipping what is other than God']. Seldom are his devotions—fasting, prayer, etc.—ever accepted.[A]

With respect to ritual duties like praying and fasting, the intention behind the act must not be adulterated with any other purpose besides pleasing God. But while that is fine for someone hard at prayer, it seems a little facile in other zones of intentionality, whether on an individual or purely collective scale. Living the life of worship through proper intentions and sincerity is not a simple affair under the best of circumstances. In the absence of a balance (*mizān*) with which to weigh or some measure by which to compare on the basis of prior knowledge, one can easily stray from the 'straight path'. That is because the limited faculties that come into play in human reasoning—no less than in ratiocination—*sensed away*, as it were, the objective concreteness which man is accustomed to and expects when 'perceiving' any reality he chooses to consider.

This may sound paradoxical or self-contradictory, but to Ghazālī and the medieval thinkers in general, reason had at some point to detach itself from the lower senses. The faculties and senses were not only susceptible to error; they also made man beholden to his own discrete perceptions, which he tended to take for the object itself. To the rational philosopher-physician Abū Bakr Rāzī (*c.* d. 936), indeed, the detachments of the rational faculty itself may cause melancholy and other ailments of the soul when taken to excess.

Clearly, Ghazālī entertained another concept of 'reason' than this, one neither inextricably tied to the human faculties (in the manner of modern psychologism) nor divorced from the practical expression of faith. It was closer to what the *falāsifa* meant by *taʿaqqul*, or intellection. We will not venture further into either

[A] Ghazālī A, 185; B, 52.

the historic or philosophic significance of this idea, except to say that it paved the way for a new vista of knowledge that has persisted until relatively recently. This is why it is so hard to classify Ghazālī at this historical juncture.

From an experiential perspective, at least, the only remaining escape from the prison of the senses was by way of self-purification. If intention is said to confer unitary focus upon human activity, then its purification allowed for the proper exteriorisation of human activity.[A] To Ghazālī, thus, intention and sincerity gave worship full reign to shape human life as it ought to be on the basis of the root source of all knowledge.

An early mystic once declared that he preferred to have an intention for everything he did—for food, drink, sleep, the lavatory.[B] Strictly speaking, none of these needs can be filled by ritual. They spring from the physical nature common to all human beings; yet they are no less significant for it. Ghazālī believed in their power either to distance one from God or to draw one closer. Thus, eating 'protected' one's acts of worship, just as the sexual act fortified one's religion. Procreation gratified the heart of family members, and begetting a godfearing child helped increase the community of believers.[C] The perfect servant of God was obedient not only in prayer and ritual, but in food and wedlock, as well, where the most perfidious of the self's pleasures lurked.[D] In that, Ghazālī was saying nothing particularly daring. Exoteric jurists and theologians taught that any means which prolonged the survival of the body and freed the heart from bodily needs constituted an aid to religion. Absent purpose or intention, which they meticulously defined, and there may be no end to overindulgence.

[A] The human act may be understood as an exteriorisation from the hidden recesses of the 'soul'. Besides the physical realm, this may include the exteriorisation of thought, articulation and so forth.

[B] *Qūt* 2:154.

[C] Ghazālī, A, 171; B, 26.

[D] *Ibid.*, A, 172; B, 27.

As Muḥyi al-Dīn Ibn ʿArabī wrote, 'Since man cannot stop desiring, the first thing that this detracts from are his acts of obedience, which he then performs without an intention (*niyya*) as set down in religious law—hence, they are not acts of obedience.[A] Ghazālī pointed out the obverse, as well, 'The way to acquire this intention surely is...to strengthen one's faith through the injunctions of religion.'[B]

Ironically, this picture leads one to think of him as a philosopher speaking down to the theologians from the perch of the logical syllogism. Perhaps this is the best way to picture his career as a thinker. Modern writers' usual portrayal of him as someone bent on slaying 'philosophy' in its berth belies the fertile complexity of the motifs that animate even his didactic works, which motifs continued to inspire thinkers long after his passing. We do polyglot thinkers of Ghazālī's calibre a disservice when we consign them to this or that 'branch of thought', or to any narrow 'religious' concept of Islam.

Some Terms and their Relationships

ʿIbāda ('servanthood', 'worship') is so encompassing that it can refer to the very act of existing. Incidentally, 'existing' was not construed as an inert state with no active or causal relation to the world even by the *falāsifa*. 'To exist' was to 'glorify', in different parlance. Later, this at least was the explicit sense in which most thinking after Ibn ʿArabī and Qūnawī deliberately moved. The Qur'ān states, *None in the heavens and earth comes to the Merciful but as a servant* (Q.XIX.93); and, *Let all that is in the heavens and the earth glorify God* (Q.LVII.1). These two verses have been cited through the ages to illustrate the Qur'ān's comprehensive view of life. Creation and all its contents are not only part of God's design but are governed by their *relationship* to the Creator, which relationship takes the

[A] Ibn ʿArabī, *al-Futūḥāt al-makkiyya*, II:687.

[B] Ghazālī A, 174; B, 30.

active verbalized (i.e., exteriorizing) form of glorification of God the Creator.

These elements obviously modified the semantics of terms like 'existent', one of Ibn Sīnā 'primary concepts'. 'To exist' somehow came to signify to face or point in a direction. The articulation of existence, which of course remained a mystery locked under the attribute of God's hiddenness, was compared to the unfolding of a book by virtue of a divine act of creation that brought all things into being. Such a delimiting but, at the same time, plenary sense easily accommodated 'worship', where any created being may be conceived of as 'worshipping', whether it is animate or inanimate. Ibn ʿArabī made a point of stressing precisely this point, as if to dispel its usual omission.[A] Nothing was without life, because 'there is not a thing that does not extol God with His praise...nor any that praises except the living. Therefore, every thing is alive.'[B] The Qur'ān supports this: *And there is not a thing but extols Him His praise* (Q. XVII.44). Dr. Suʿād al-Ḥakīm offers a useful representation of the reasoning behind this:

Premise 1: Every thing (*shay'*) extols God's praises.
Premise 2: All that praise are alive
Conclusion: Every thing is alive.[C]

Ibn ʿArabī wanted to elucidate the causative emanation of life, where furthermore, 'sensations and the senses are something intellected (*maʿqūl*) that is added to the fact that the being is alive.'[D] And he was careful not to muddle matters of morality and responsibility at this elementary level, where life is innate and pre-given—unlike the Stoics, who interpreted 'cause' (*aiton*) according to its

[A] In Ibn ʿArabī's expansive view of innate life (*al-ḥayāt al-fiṭriyya*), life permeated all existent things: man, animal, plant and even mineral (Ibn ʿArabī, *al-Futūḥāt al-makkiyya*, III, 490-1).

[B] *Fuṣūṣ al-ḥikam*, I, 170.

[C] *Al-Muʿjam al- ṣūfī*, 364.

[D] *Al-Futūḥāt al-makkiyya*, III, 324.

etymology. Morality presupposed a *sentient* rational living being using his senses for various purposes. 'Life' eluded us whenever we try to observe it in the created things around us, he explained, because we assume that it is conditional upon sensation.[A] But the truth about 'life' lay elsewhere. What distinguished human 'worship' from its analogues elsewhere in creation was the purposefulness with which man acted, always with the assistance of his erring but indispensable faculties.

The Prophet taught that deeds had to be performed through intention and reckoning *because* one must act deliberately in faith, ablutions, prayer, almsgiving, pilgrimage, fasting and the divine commands.[B] This connects intentionality as such with the symbolic manifestation of human activity as such in the more specific and deliberate act of worship called ritual. According to Sufyān al-Thawrī, the early Muslims 'learned intention in order to act as well as they learned to act'.[C] Among other things, how could 'acting' be deliberate, the way it should to be, without the use of the human faculties in learning? But how could there be learning without the transference of prior knowledge in the first place?

This view locates both intention and learning no doubt squarely in the fold of life's tasks, not just the symbolic ritual, but it also makes for the compatibility and mutual enrichment of the rational and religious sciences, as Ghazālī himself observed.

Niyya (intention) literally means 'to head towards a place different from where one is now, or intending an action'.[D] The Prophet is reported to have said, 'To every man his intention. He who migrates for God and His Messenger does so for God and His Messenger. But he who migrates for a world to gain or a woman

[A] *Ibid.*

[B] Bukhārī, '*Mā jā'a inna al-aʿmāl bil-niyya wa'l-ḥisba*' 1:37, no. 52.

[C] *Ibid.* Instead of 'as well as they learned *to act*', Makkī wrote 'as well as they learned *knowledge*'.

[D] *Lisān al-ʿarab* 15:348.

to wed migrates to whatever he migrates to.'[A] While conscious intention is more easily grasped in the familiar terms of daily life than in the well-kneaded conceptions of the dialecticians and the philosophers, its intrinsic 'directionality' gives it an inescapable eschatological dimension, such that the fate of human beings ultimately rests on intention. This is confirmed by scriptural sources, including a tradition that says, 'They shall be resurrected according to their intentions.'[B]

All this could not but put a premium on the act of purification. Ḥasan al-Baṣrī, instrumental in setting the intellectual tone of reflections on doctrine and ethics early on, taught that intention and its purification of all vainglorious things were essential to action.[C] 'By their intentions,' he said, 'the people of Paradise live everlastingly in the Garden and the people of Hellfire dwell in the Fire.'[D] But intention was also prior to action. This position, in particular, has a certain precedent dating back to a well-known tradition of the Prophet, to the effect that actions were dependent on intention.[E] That the intention should be both prior and 'better' than action in this sense,[F] Ghazālī pointed out, was visible only to those who understood the true purpose and scope of 'religion'.

This rudimentary way of considering 'priority' echoed Ibn Sīnā's treatment of this concept, which is so fundamental to philosophic thinking and which Yaḥyā Suhrawardī al-Maqtūl in turn refined. That said, Ghazālī insisted on balancing intention against action because, as a general rule, it cannot completely supplant action.

[A] Bukhārī, Īmān , 1:2, no. 1; Muslim, *Imāra*, 3:33, no. 155; Ibn Ḥanbal 1:25; Ibn Māja, *K. al-zuhd*, 2:1413, no. 4227. Cf. Zabīdī's commentary on this tradition (10:67).

[B] Ibn Ḥanbal 3:311, 319, 338, 371; *Qūt* 2:161; cf. Irāqī 157.

[C] Massignon, *Essai* 186.

[D] *Qūt* 2:160.

[E] Ibn Māja, *K. al-zuhd*, 2:1413, no. 4227.

[F] *Lisān al-ʿarab* 15:348.

Intention came also to be variously defined in terms of 'will', 'the purpose in the heart' and, according to Taymī, 'the aim of the heart'.[A] Bayḍāwī explained it as the 'actuation of the heart towards what it considers useful or away from what it considers harmful'; and Zabīdī as 'will aiming towards action and desiring God's countenance.'[B] Changing the intention modified the will's focus and, thus, the action flowing from it. Talk of 'priority' would seem unintelligible otherwise. Very often intention was used synonymously with 'purpose', or *qaṣd*. However, for Jāḥiẓ, an early *mutakallim*, purpose was a type of knowing—in other words, there was purpose 'when the agent was not unconscious'; the person had to be conscious of what he or she was doing.[C] Needless to say, this formulation fails to clarify what intention does. It may help to note that, unlike *niyya*, the word *qaṣd* figures in the Qur'ān. It was widely used in the exegetical literature to signal the proper method of interpreting a given passage according to the *purpose* of God, or some interest therein. As a practical and moral act, by contrast, 'intending' referred to the motivational source of man's external behaviour. This was true not just in the case of *ritual* acts of worship, but in any act of worship. By the same token, any act of worship bereft of intention whatsoever was said to be void.[D] As a ritual, prayer (*ṣalāt*) recapitulated and offered up to God the whole range of a supplicant's life in symbolic fashion. Ritual also symbolised human agency, as we said, which paradoxically can only be borrowed from on high, learned only by way of submission to the Lord, or *Rabb al-ʿālamīn*. Therefore, if life is a prayer to the Creator—a theme on which Henry Corbin expanded creatively—then how

[A] Ibrāhīm b. Yazīdī b. al-Ḥārith al-Taymī (d. 92/710-11), an ascetic from Kufa who followed an austere form of spiritual discipline. Al-Ḥajjāj imprisoned him and had him killed at forty years old. (Abū Nuʿaym 4:210-19; Dhahabī, *Tadhkīrāt* 1:73, no. 69; Nabhānī 1:384-5).

[B] Zabīdī, *Itiḥāf* 10:26.

[C] Daniel Gimaret, *Théorie de l'acte humain en théologie musulmane* 35.

[D] As Ibn Rushd notes, religious scholars agree on the requirement of intention in every act of worship (*Bidāyat al-mujtahid* 6).

could one action engender another without the unifying focus of a purified intention and exercise of the will to fulfil it? Action in that case would be meaningless—or worse, stillborn.

Sālim b. ʿAbd Allāh[A] once wrote to ʿUmar b. ʿAbd al-ʿAzīz, 'Know that God's succour to man is in proportion to his intention. Therefore, God's succour is complete for that person whose intention is complete, and incomplete as the latter is incomplete.'[B] Theologically, this meant that 'God establishes the habit of creating every act the acquisition of which man intends. When God wants to create in man a free movement...He creates in him such a movement only if man wants it, chooses it and *intends* to acquire it,' if one accepts Naṣafī's stipulation.[C]

On these issues—complex as they are even against an anecdotal background of sayings and reports about intention, which abound in the literature of the period—suffice it to say that intention stood on a human choice which either agreed with God's purpose or did not, *prior* to (though not necessarily 'before', in the temporal sense) any action taking place. Here, Ghazālī determined, intention to be simply the soul's motive, orientation and inclination towards what the soul construed as its purpose within the bounds of this world and relative to the next. 'For the person whose intention is the world, God shall put his poverty before his very eyes. [That person] shall part with it [i.e., the world] with the greatest desire for it. As for the one whose intention is the Hereafter, God shall put his wealth in his heart and hold him to his estate. He will part with it, fully renouncing it.'[D]

All told, the human act—in both movement and rest (based on the fundamental physics of the time)—contained three elements:

[A] Sālim b. ʿAbd Allāh [d. 106/724] was one of the seven leading *fuqahā'* in his time. He was respected for his good judgment and religious steadfastness (Zabīdī 10:11).

[B] Cf. Ibn Ḥanbal 5:446.

[C] Gimaret, *Théorie de l'acte humain en théologie musulmane*, 207.

[D] Ibn Māja, *K. al-zuhd*, 2:1375, no. 4105; Qūt 2:161.

knowledge, will and power. Ghazālī assumed that knowledge too was prior to action, being its root and condition; whereas action was the fruit and branch. For, man could not desire what he did not know, nor could he act without willing.[A] In order to act man needed a motive; here, three components come to the fore: the actuating mover (goal sought), motivating goal (purpose intended) and actuation (intention and will). In this scheme, intention was an intermediary attribute connected to the will and the actuation of the soul consonance with the value of its desire for whatever agreed with the goal.

It is not for nothing that Ghazālī called intention the very 'spirit' of action (*rūh al-ʿamal*), in the sense of a *causal living* source of the act, as indeed the attribute of power—which man shares with God—entailed. Everyone from Ghazālī to Mullā Ṣadrā conceived of life as the 'life of faith', as well as a name for the sensory/motor powers of all animate beings. This was quite in keeping with the classical *kalām* approach to analogical reasoning and, to some extent, that of *falsafa*. So long as the heart was moved to action, nevertheless, the concepts of 'action' and 'movement' could not well maintain the bare-bone character they acquired, say, in Ibn Sīnā's physics, which was merely preparatory for what moved bodies. Without the *proper* and *conscious* intention, action was either rudderless or a mere pretence. Intention could not be reduced to a blithe uttering of 'I intend'—i.e., declared only 'with the tongue;'[B] it was as good as one's fidelity to God's purpose, even in the event where an obstacle should hinder the commission of the act. Faith gave concrete human expression to this intention, because the life of faith—as indeed, all life—originated with God, the Eternally Living (*al-Ḥayy*) and the Giver of Life (*al-Muḥyī*).

The Arabic saying that reads, 'Seek the intention of the act before the act [itself], and you shall have the good insofar as you intend the good,' offers a slightly different variation. For, how

[A] Ghazālī A, 159; B, 12.
[B] *Ibid.*, A, 175; B, 31.

should one judge goodness? Naturally, on the basis of scripture and both the living and recorded authorities of the Prophet's *Sunna*. But Ghazālī also enriched the prevailing view of the necessary learning through *taqlīd*, as on so many other issues, precisely by pointing to what the 'forefathers' (*al-salaf*) of the Muslim community taught about the sincerity of purposeful action toward the betterment of deeds. According to him, they held that through sincerity intention had the power to increase a small deed or to lessen a great one.[A] But only where there was a single motive could the act that sprang from intention be said to be *sincere*—i.e., relative to what is intended.[B] This is why he combined the themes of sincerity (*ikhlāṣ*) and truthfulness (*ṣidq*) in this book.

And still, sincerity was not enough, for Abū Yaʿqūb al-Sūsī[C] was reported to have said, 'Sincerity precludes seeing sincerity. The person who sees sincerity in his sincerity needs to purify his sincerity'; 'The act which is truly sincere is that which is known neither by an angel to record it; nor by any devil to corrupt it; nor by the soul to take pride in it.'[D] Granted, sincerity—strictly speaking—could only be sincerity of intention, a quality many Sufis regarded as a 'rarity';[E] it nevertheless signified that a personal act has reconciled the living agent's 'exterior' (*ẓāhir*) with the 'interior' (*bāṭin*);[F] meaning that no temptation or hypocrisy impinged on the behaviour.[G] Ghazālī's commentator, Zabīdī, likened sincerity to *al-ʿurwa al-wuthqa*,[H] 'the firmest grasp' mentioned in the Qur'ān—*Truth stands out clear from error: whoever*

[A] *Qūt* 2:159.

[B] Ghazālī A, 183; B, 50.

[C] Abū Yaʿqūb Isḥāq b. Muḥammad al-Sūsī al-Nahrajūrī [d. 336/947] was a sage from Nahrajūr. He lived in Basra and Baghdad as a follower of Junayd (Jāmī 1:129-30, no. 139).

[D] Kalābādhī, *The Doctrine of the Sūfis* 91.

[E] Qushayrī, *Risāla* 164, q.v. '*Ikhlāṣ*'.

[F] Zabīdī 10:65.

[G] *Ibid.*

[H] Zabīdī 10:42.

rejects evil and believes in God hath held the firmest gasp that never breaks.[A]

As a concept, truthfulness, which also figures in the title of Ghazālī's book, is closely allied to sincerity. Basing himself on Qushayrī, Jurjānī held that one was truthful 'when situations are unblemished, beliefs have no doubt, actions have no shame.'[B] Ghazālī further distinguished six senses: truthfulness in speech, intention and will; in resolve; in the fulfilment of resolve; in action; in the realisation of every religious station. Someone who is ascribed all of these was 'perfectly truthful', or *ṣiddīq*, this being the most intense form of truthfulness.[C]

Sources

Two manuscripts were used for this translation. The first is the Cairo edition, which contains the notes of Zayn al-Dīn al-ʿIrāqī (1404 CE), is referred to as Ms A in the notes. The second edition (Ms B) is the one used in the lengthy commentary of the erudite eighteenth-century scholar, Muḥammad b. Muḥammad al-Ḥusayn al-Zabīdī, more commonly known as Murtaḍā Zabīdī (1791 CE).

Many thanks to Dr. Eric Ormsby for suggesting, nearly fifteen years ago, inside his office stacked ceiling-high with books, that I speak with the Islamic Texts Society about their ongoing Ghazali series. I have availed myself of the Zabidi volumes he kindly lent me for this and the two other translations in the series. I had barely begun to hear about ITS then, and was quickly surprised. I want to express my deepest gratitude to Fatima Azzam, the Director, for her outstanding work as editor and boundless patience. She has contributed generously in several ways to the manuscript, including in the thankless business of annotation.

A Q. 2.256; 31.22.

B Jurjānī, *Taʿrīfāt*, 132.

C Ghazālī, A, 197; B, 72.

While her special touch, exceptional skills and mastery of the Arabic language have brought significant improvements to the original text, I have especially enjoyed intellectual exchange with a person of intimate, well-rounded knowledge of the Islamic heritage. All of which, of course, translates into a writer's dream. Translation being an artist's art, nevertheless, despite my best efforts, I must remind the reader that anything unseemly or erroneous in the final outcome is fully mine.

THE BOOK OF INTENTION, SINCERITY AND TRUTHFULNESS

Being the Seventh Book of the Quarter
of Saving Virtues

[PROLOGUE]

In the Name of God, the Merciful, the Compassionate

WE PRAISE GOD in the manner of the grateful, and believe in Him in the manner of those who are certain of faith, and we affirm His oneness in the manner of the truthful. We bear witness that there is no deity save God, Lord of the Worlds, Creator of the heavens and the earth—who charged *jinn* and man and the archangels to worship Him with sincerity. Said God, *They were commanded only to worship God in sincere devotion to Him.*[1] To God belongs none but firm, sincere religion, for He is the least needful of any partnership with compeers.

And blessings be upon His prophet, Muḥammad, leader of His messengers; upon all the prophets and upon Muḥammad's household and his Companions good and pure.

Now, men of heart have discovered through the insight of faith and the luminances of the Qur'ān that happiness is attainable only by knowledge (*ʿilm*) and worship (*ʿibāda*). Consequently, all people shall perish save the knowing, and all the knowing shall perish save those who act, and all those who act shall perish except the sincere. But the sincere face an awesome danger. For action (*ʿamal*) without intention (*niyya*) is drudgery, whereas intention without sincerity (*ikhlāṣ*) is ostentation, and that is equivalent to hypocrisy and the same as disobedience. Sincerity without truthfulness (*ṣidq*) and exactitude (*taḥqīq*) is but a scatter of dust. God said that every act intended[A] for any but God is tarnished and soiled—*And We shall turn to what deeds they have done, and all about We shall make these deeds a scatter of dust.*[2]

I wish I knew how someone ignorant of the reality of intention could attest to his own intention; or how someone ignorant of the reality of sincerity could attest to sincerity. How can someone sincerely claim truthfulness for himself if he has not confirmed its reality?

The first task of every human being who desires to obey God is to learn intention; firstly, in order to obtain knowledge, then, so he may prove it through action after understanding the reality of truthfulness and sincerity, which are the two ways for the worshipper to salvation and deliverance. We shall indicate the meaning of truthfulness and sincerity in three parts:

Part One: The reality of intention and its meaning;
Part Two: Sincerity and its reality;
Part Three: Truthfulness and its reality.

[A] Ghazālī used the word *irāda* (will or the act of will), which is important to keep in mind when considering 'power' and speech. These issues originated in *Kalām*, which is frequently in the background with Ghazālī.

PART I

ON INTENTION

In it is an exposition of the merit of intention, an exposition of the reality of intention, an exposition of the superiority of intention over action, a classification of how actions are related to intention and an exposition whereby intention is not a matter of choice.

CHAPTER ONE

An Exposition of the Merit of Intention

GOD HAS SAID, *Do not turn away those who call on their Lord morning and evening, wishing for His countenance.*[1] What is meant by this wishing is intention. The Prophet (may God bless him and grant him peace) said, 'Verily, deeds are [performed] with intentions. To every man[2] his intention. He who migrates for God and His Messenger, does so for God and His Messenger. But he who migrates for a world to gain or a woman to wed, migrates to whatever he migrates to.'[3]

The Prophet also said, 'Most of the martyrs in my community lay in their berths.[A] While many a man who has fallen between the two rows, only God knows his intention.'[4] God said, *If they intend reconciliation, God will grant them both success.*[5] Thus, God made intention the cause of success (*tawfīq*).

Said the Prophet, 'God (Exalted is He) sees neither your forms nor your riches, but your hearts and deeds.'[6] God sees the hearts because they are the loci of intention.

May God bless him and grant him peace said, 'The servant [of God] performs good deeds, which the angels raise up on sealed scrolls. These are laid before God, who says, "Cast this scroll away, for by what is in it he intended not My countenance." And with that He calls on the angels, "Write for him such-and-such, and write such-and-such." They say, "Our Lord, he did none of these things." But God shall answer, "He intended them."'[7]

[A] That is, they died honourably (cf. Zabīdī 10).

Said the Prophet, 'There are four kinds of people: To one man God Almighty gives knowledge and wealth, and he acts knowledgeably with his wealth. And a man says, "Would that God (Exalted is He) had given me what He has given him, for I would do as he does." Both men are equally recompensed. [Then,] there is the man to whom God (Exalted is He) gives wealth but not knowledge. He gropes about with his wealth. And a man says, "Would that God had given me what He has given him, for I would do as he does." Therefore, they are equally in error.'[8] Do you not see how, in his good and evil acts, he shares the intention [of the other man]?

Likewise in a tradition of Anas b. Mālik. When the Messenger of God embarked on the Tabūk campaign, he said, 'There are many in Medina who, while still in the city, are joined with us in every valley we have crossed, every path we trod that vexed the unfaithful, every provision spent or hunger felt.' They asked, 'How could it be, O Messenger of God, if they were not with us?' He said, 'They were excusably detained'[9]—and partook by way of good intention.

In a tradition of Ibn Masᶜūd, 'He who migrates in search of something shall find it.[10] A man took one of our womenfolk in marriage and was named the Migrant of Umm Qays.'[A][11]

Also, a report relates that a man who died in the path of God was named 'Felled for a Donkey',[B] because he had fought another man for booty and his donkey. This was added to his intention.[12]

According to a tradition narrated by ᶜIbāda [b. Ṣāmit], the Prophet said, 'He who fights with the intention only to have his share [of the booty] shall have only what he intends.'[13]

[Ibn ᶜIbāda] further said that his father[C] had said, 'I sought the help of a man who fought with me. He said, "Only if you pay me a reward." Therefore, I paid him. I mentioned this to the Prophet, who said, "He has nothing in this world and the next save what you paid him."'[14]

[A] *Muhājir Umm Qays*, an Arabian tribe.

[B] *Qatīl al-ḥimār*.

[C] His father was Ibn Kaᶜb (Zabīdī 8).

According to an Israelite story, a man came upon a sand dune during a famine and said to himself, 'If only this sand were food, I would have apportioned it among the people.' God inspired their prophet to tell [this man] that God accepts his alms, thanks his good intention and grants him the reward for something which, had it been food, he would have offered as alms.[15]

In many reports it is said, 'A good deed is recorded for the person who means to perform a good deed but does not.'[16]

A tradition narrated by ʿAbd Allāh b. Ibn ʿUmar, 'For the person whose intention is the world, God shall put his poverty before his very eyes. [That person] shall part with it with the greatest desire for it. And for the one whose intention is the Hereafter, God shall put his wealth in his heart and return him what he had lost. [That person] will part with it, fully renouncing it.'[17]

In a tradition narrated by Umm Salama,[A] the Prophet once spoke of an army whom the desert had swallowed up. 'I asked him, "O Messenger of God, [but] among them are both the enforcers and the hirelings."[B] He said, "They shall be resurrected according to their intentions."'[18]

ʿUmar stated that he heard God's Messenger say, 'Fighters fight according to intentions.'[19]

The Prophet (may God bless him and grant him peace) said, 'When the two rows meet, the angels descend to record men their ranks: so-and-so fought for the world; so-and-so fought zealously; so-and-so fought for clan. Therefore, say not that this person fell in the path of God, for only he who fights to make God's word supreme is on God's path.'[20]

On the authority of Jābir [b. ʿAbd Allāh al-Anṣarī], it is related that the Messenger of God said, 'Every servant of God is resurrected according to that for which he died.'[21]

[A] Umm Salama (d. 62/681) was a wife of the Prophet Muḥammad.

[B] That is, those who led the army and were responsible for the calamity that befell them, and those who served only as hirelings.

In the tradition of al-Aḥnaf [al-Qays al-Tamīmī], from Abū Bakra, [God's Messenger declares], 'When two Muslims draw swords, both the killer and the killed shall be in the Fire.' The Messenger was then asked, 'It is so for the killer, but why the one killed?' He said, 'Because he sought to kill his fellow [Muslim].'[22]

According to a tradition narrated by Abū Hurayra, 'He is an adulterer who takes a woman in marriage on a dowry which he has no intention of fulfilling. And he is a thief who takes on a debt which he has no intention of repaying.'[23]

Said the Messenger (may God bless him and grant him peace), 'He who perfumes himself for God (Exalted is He) shall go forth on the Day of Resurrection with a scent more fragrant than that of musk. He who perfumes himself for any other shall go forth on the Day of Resurrection with an odour more putrid than that of carrion.'[24]

The Narratives (Āthār)[A]

ᶜUmar b. al-Khaṭṭāb (may God be pleased with him) said that the best deeds are the fulfilment of what God (Exalted is He) has enjoined, fear of what God has forbidden and truthfulness of intention with respect to God.[25]

Sālim b. ᶜAbd Allāh once wrote to ᶜUmar b. ᶜAbd al-ᶜAzīz, 'Know that God's succour to man is in proportion to his intention. Therefore, God's succour is complete for that person whose intention is complete, and incomplete as the latter is incomplete.'[26]

One of the forefathers [*Salaf*] said, 'Intention may aggrandise a small deed or lessen a great deed.'[27]

And Dā'ūd al-Ṭā'ī said, 'The devout person is intently god-fearing. Therefore, even if he were attached by every limb to this world, his very intention would one day return him to the sound intention. The ignorant person is, however, the opposite of this.'[28]

[A] Reports not connected with the Prophet.

Said [Sufyān] al-Thawrī, 'They learned intention in order to act, just as well as they learned to act.'[29]

Said one of the learned, 'Seek the intention of the act before the act [itself]. You shall have the good insofar as you intend the good.'[30]

A [Sufi] novice used to go around the learned asking, 'Who will show me work by which I shall always be working for God (Exalted is He), for I loathe to pass an hour of the day or the night[31] save as one of God's workers.' He was told, 'You have realised your wish. Do what good you can. If you slacken or abandon it [altogether], then set your mind to its performance, because setting one's mind to [performing] the good is like performing it.'[32]

Similarly, one of the forefathers once said, 'Verily, God's blessings upon you are greater than you can reckon; your sins are lesser than you know. Yet repent by day and by night, and [God] will pardon you what lies between the two.'[A][33]

And Jesus (peace be upon him) said, 'Blessed is the eye that neither sleeps perturbed by any offence nor wakens to any sin.'[34]

Said Abū Hurayra, 'They will be gathered on the Day of Resurrection according to the measure of their intentions.'[35]

Al-Fuḍayl b. ᶜIyaḍ used to weep whenever he heard, *And We shall try you to learn who among you strives and forebears, and We shall test [the sincerity] of your assertions.*[36] He was wont to repeat it and to say, 'When You put us to trial, You put us to shame; You reave away our veils.'[37]

Said al-Ḥasan [al-Baṣrī], 'By their intentions, the people of Paradise live everlastingly in the Garden and the people of hellfire dwell in the Fire.'[38]

Abū Hurayra said, 'It is written in the Torah, "What is intended for Me is ample, be it small. What is intended for another is small, be it ample."'[39]

Bilāl b. Saᶜd [b. Tamīm al-Ashᶜarī] said that the servant may utter the word of a believer, but God (Exalted is He) will not

[A] That is, between the day and the night.

leave him or his word be until He sees his deed. When the servant acts, God will not leave him until He sees his piety. If he becomes pious, [God] will not leave him until He sees whatever he had intended. Thus, when his intention is sound everything below it cannot but be sound.[40]

Therefore, the [very] pillar[A] of action is intention, and the deed depends on intention[41] and through it becomes good. Intention [remains] good in itself even if the act were impeded by an obstacle.

[A] ‘*ʿImād*’ conjures the image of pillar, but Ghazālī intends a stronger sense here, closer perhaps to ‘bastion’.

CHAPTER TWO

An Exposition of the Reality of Intention

KNOW THAT INTENTION (*niyya*), will (*irāda*) and purpose (*qaṣd*) are synonymous terms with a single connotation, which is a state and an attribute of the heart bound by two things: knowledge and action. Knowledge is prior to action, being its root and condition. Action follows because it is the fruit and branch. This is because every free action—I mean every movement and rest—is incomplete without three things: knowledge (*ʿilm*), will (*irāda*) and power (*qudra*). For man has no desire for what he does not know. He *must* know. Nor can he act without willing. Therefore, there must be a will.

Will signifies the rousing of the heart towards what it thinks accords with [its] goal, be it present or future. Man was created such that one thing suits him and is congruous with his goals while another is incompatible with him. He needs to attract towards him that which is congruous and suitable and to repel what is baneful and unsuitable for him.

Therefore, he needs perforce to know and to distinguish the harmful from the beneficial thing, attracting this and repelling that. It is not within the capacity of someone who has never seen or known food to consume it; and it is not within the capacity of someone who has not seen fire to flee it. Consequently, God has created guidance (*hidāya*) and cognisance (*maʿrifa*)[A] and devised the

[A] *Maʿrifa*, like *ʿilm*, may translate as 'knowledge'. It refers to knowledge, apprehension or cognisance but at the level of the *psyche*. This does not necessarily imply that a *ʿārif* (cognisant subject; knower) may only avail himself

means to obtain them—namely, the outer and inner senses.[A] But this is not our object [of inquiry].

Now, even if one were to see food and to know that it is suitable for one, this would be insufficient so long as one lacks the inclination for it or the desire or appetite to induce him. For an ailing person may see food and know that it is suitable for him but yet be incapable of eating it, since no desire or inclination exists, nor is there an actuating motive.

God (Exalted is He) creates in him inclination, desire and will, and by that I mean a longing for it in him and a leaning towards it in his heart. But this, too, is insufficient for him. For how many a person who eyes food desires it, wants to consume it but is incapable of this because he is infirm! Therefore, power and limb movement were created for him that he may manage to eat. No bodily member can move without power; and power awaits the actuating

of the limited human faculties of perception, or that there is only the private experience of knowing at this level. Nevertheless, the term makes more sense from the 'psychological' epistemology which many thinkers at the time expressed in terms of the inner and outer senses (as indeed the author himself does below). Jurjānī explains that, unlike the term *ʿālim* (knower), the *ʿārif* (cognisant subject; knower) cannot be applied to God, since *maʿrifa* also suggests a state of ignorance before the knowledge (Jurjānī, *Taʿrīfāt*, 221). Whereas *ʿilm* (knowledge) is an 'imitable' divine attribute, *maʿrifa* refers to that knowledge which we possess, together with understanding, comprehension, familiarity, etc. But *ʿilm* and *ʿālim* may equally refer to science and scholar, respectively, neither of which would however make sense when considered only in terms of private experience. In an allied sense, *maʿrifa* can connote a grasp of such a science. Both *ʿilm* and *maʿrifa* have technical and nontechnical uses, and the main difference between them has to do with which aspect of knowledge is under consideration. In this primary respect, *maʿrifa* is connected with the *reception* of knowledge; *ʿilm* refers to knowledge as such and may apply to both God and human beings.

[A] The inner senses consist of the retentive imagination, composite animal and human imagination, estimation, memory and the common sense—with certain variations from one medieval thinker and tradition to the other. The outer, physical senses are hearing, seeing, touch, etc.

motive; while the motive awaits either knowledge and cognisance or opinion and belief—thereby strengthening the suitability of something inside him.

When cognisance determines that something is suitable and must be done, and that it is unfettered by another, contrary motive directing away from [the thing], then the will is actuated and the inclination realised. When the will is actuated, the power is roused (*intahaḍat*) to move the members.[1] Power thus serves[2] the will, which in turn follows the precept[A] of belief and knowledge.

Intention, then, is an intermediary attribute. It consists of the will and the motivation of the self through the precept of the desire and the inclination for whatever agrees with the goal—be it present or future.

The first mover is the sought-after goal, being the motive (*bāʿith*). The motivating goal (*gharaḍ bāʿith*) is the intended purpose. The motivation is the resolve and intention. The rousing of the power to assist the will in moving the members is the act. However, rousing the power to act may happen through a single motive; it may also happen through two motives joined in a single act. If there are two motives, then each could separately rouse the power. [Or,] neither may be capable of this unless [both motives are] joined; [or] one may be sufficient without the other, even when the other is roused to its support and assistance.

[A] *Ḥukm* usually translates as 'precept'. The *Shorter Oxford Dictionary* defines 'precept' as general instruction, command, rule for action, maxim; a direction for the performance of a technical operation, etc. This seems to agree with the Arabic *ḥukm*, which does not translate well into the more literal 'ruling' or 'judgment' in every context. Nothing keeps us from attaching a distinct meaning to an existing English term. Jurjānī defined *ḥukm* as 'the positing of a thing at its proper place' (*Taʿrīfāt* 92). In this epistemological sense, the precept governs other determinations lying below it. This gives the term wide-ranging application and includes the act of judging something concerning something else, yielding the relational complex of 'judge', 'what is judged upon' and 'judgment'. This is exactly how some later mystics have analysed *ḥukm* (Ṣadr al-Dīn Qūnawī's *Kitāb al-nuṣūṣ* is a good example).

From this division four classes [of motive] emerge. Let us give a name and an example to each one:

Firstly, a single motive, alone and exclusive—as when a wild animal attacks a man. Upon seeing the animal, the man quickly displaces himself, his only concern being to escape the animal. Therefore, he sees this wild animal and recognises it as dangerous. He is motivated to escape and desires it. Hence, power is roused to act according to the motivation. And of the person it is said that his intention is to flee the wild animal, not to embark on anything else. The name for this intention is 'pure', and by the same token acting upon it is called sincerity (*ikhlāṣ*) with respect to the motivating goal. This means that it is free of association with anything else or adulteration.

Secondly, the two motives are combined, [although] each one could, alone and independently, rouse [the power]. A concrete example[A] of this is when two men help each other carry something with the measure of power of only one. For our purpose, an example of this is when a person is asked for something by his poor kin and complies on account of the latter's poverty and kinship. He knows that had his kin not been poor, he would have complied solely out of kinship; and that[3] had he not been a kin, he would have complied for reason of poverty alone. He would know this on his own because he [usually] fulfils the request of a wealthy kin and the need of a poor stranger alike.

It is the same for a person whom the physician has ordered to avoid food. Fasting on the day of ʿArafa, he knows well that even without the day of ʿArafa he would have avoided food for dietary reasons;[B] and absent his diet, he would still have avoided

[A] *Mithāl min al-maḥsūs*—lit., a tangible example.

[B] The day of ʿArafa (*yawm ʿArafa*) is the ninth day of the month of Dhū al-Ḥijja and the most important day of the annual pilgrimage to Mecca. It is so-called because of, it is said, the reconnoitering of people (*yataʿārifūna*) at the site of ʿArafa. *Yataʿārifūna* has the same root as *ʿArafa* (cf. *Lisān al-ʿArab* IX:242). While pilgrims fast on the day of ʿArafa, fasting is not obligatory. Legend has

the food because it is the day of ʿArafa. But the [two motives] were joined together and he embarked on the action. The second motive accompanies the first. Let us therefore name this [class of motive] the 'accompaniment of motives'.

Thirdly, none of the [motives] is sufficient by itself, but their combination can rouse the power. A concrete example of this is when two weak [men] help each other to carry what each of them alone cannot. For our purpose, an example of this is like when a man is accosted by a wealthy relative asking for a *dirham* and he gives him none. The poor stranger goes to ask him for a *dirham* and he gives him none. But when his poor kin goes to him he gives it. His actuating cause is the sum of both motives—namely, kinship and poverty. Similar is the man who gives alms in front of people for merit (*thawāb*) and praise (*thanā'*).[4] By itself the goal of merit would not motivate him to give, for if the petitioner had been sinful, there would be no reward for giving alms. Pure ostentation would not motivate him to give. But if[5] the two [motives] were joined together, their joining would cause the heart to be moved. Let us name this [class of motive] 'association'.

Fourthly, when one motive is sufficient by itself, while the second is not; yet if the latter is attached to the [the first] it cannot be dissociated from an effect by way of assistance and facilitation. A concrete example is when a weak man helps a strong man to carry [something]. By himself the strong man would be sufficient; whereas by himself the weak one would not—although together [with the strong man] he facilitates and lightens[6] the work. For our purpose, then, this is illustrated by the person in the habit of performing devotional prayers[A] and giving alms. Were a group of

it also that it was here that Adam and Eve were reunited after the Fall and where they recognised each other. Another legend is that of Abraham, with whom the Angel Gabriel was circumambulating. After showing him the spiritual sights, Gabriel asked him, 'Knowest thou, knowest thou?' And Abraham answered, 'I know, I know'—i.e., *ʿaraftu*.

[A] Additional to the five canonical prayers.

people to congregate nearby at the time [of his prayer], his deed would be lightened because of their visibility. He knows on his own that if he were alone and free, he would not slacken in his act. He also knows that had his act not been out of obedience [to God], mere ostentation would not help him carry it out as it would tarnish the intention. Let us name this class [of motive] 'assistance'.

Thus, the secondary motive may be a 'companion', an 'ally' or an 'aid'.[A] We shall evaluate these in the chapter on sincerity. Our goal now is to demonstrate the divisions of intention because actions depend on and obtain their precept (*ḥukm*) from what motivates them. This is why it is said that actions are through intentions.[7] For action is subordinate, possessing no value in itself. The value is in that to which it is subordinate.[B]

[A] These epithets appear to differ with respect not only to the closeness of the two persons, but also to the intensity of their relationship. Jurjānī rightly characterises *shirka* as a formal association, in the sense of a commercial company. A *sharīk* (or ally) is thus an associate understood in this formal sense. 'Companion' (*rafīq*), on the other hand, conveys the closest and most intense relationship. *Muʿīn* (aid) seems to intermediate between them.

[B] That is, the value is in the intention.

CHAPTER THREE

An Exposition of the Inner Meaning of the Prophet's Words: 'The intention of the believer is better than his deed'[1]

KNOW THAT THE reason for this preponderance[A] is thought to be that intention is a secret which no one but God (Exalted is He) fathoms. Action is exterior. It is true that actions done in secret are superior. Yet this is not the point here. If a person intends to invoke God in his heart or to reflect on the interests of the Muslims, then the general [understanding] of the prophetic saying [above] implies that the intention to reflect is better than the reflection [itself].

It is also thought that the reason for the preponderance is that intention[2] lasts until the end of the action, whereas actions do not persist. This [view] is weak[B] because it may imply that more action is better than less. But it is not so, for the [declared] intention of the acts of prayer lasts only for a few moments, while the acts[C] persist.

The general [affirmation of the saying] requires that the intention be better than the deed. It has been argued that this implies that the intention alone is better than the action alone without the intention. This is true—albeit still far from being

[A] That is, the preponderance in the title of the chapter; namely of intention over action.

[B] That is, this justification is valid enough but nevertheless constitutes a weak interpretation of the tradition.

[C] That is, the prayers.

the purpose—since unintended or inadvertent action contains no good by nature; whereas intention alone is good. The preponderance is obvious to anyone who subscribes to the nature of the good.

The [prophetic saying] means that every pious deed is regulated by intention and action. Intention and action are both part of a class of good deeds. Nevertheless intention as part of a class of pious deeds is better than action—i.e., both affect what is intended, although the effect of intention is greater than that of action. Therefore, [the saying] means that 'the intention of the believer' as part of the class of his pious deeds is better than his deed, which in turn is part of the class of his pious deeds. The goal is that the servant of God chooses intention and action, which are two operations. But of the two, intention is better. This is what [the tradition] means.

The reason that intention is preponderant and better than action is discernible only to one who understands the purpose and way of religion, and the range of steps along the path leading to that goal; one who compares each step with the other—until he discovers through this which one is preponderant in relation to the goal.

[For example,] he who says that bread is better than fruit means better in relation to the goal of sustenance and nourishment. This is discernible only to someone who understands that nourishment has a purpose: health and survival; and that foods vary in their effects—this person understands each and compares them with each other. Pious acts are the nourishment of the hearts—the goal is their healing, survival, welfare and felicity in the Hereafter, and luxuriating in the meeting with God (Exalted is He). The only goal is the pleasure of the meeting with God. No one will luxuriate in the meeting with God who does not die loving and knowing God. Only he loves Him who knows Him. And only he is intimate with His Lord[3] who lengthens the invocation of His [Name]; for intimacy is reached through continuous invocation.

Chapter Three

Knowledge (*maʿrifa*) is attained through continuous contemplation (*fikr*). Love necessarily follows knowledge. The heart can devote itself to continuous invocation and contemplation only if it frees itself of preoccupation with this world. It becomes free of preoccupation with it only if its desires for it cease, whereupon it becomes inclined towards the good, aspiring to it and shunning and loathing evil. Just as the reasoning person is inclined towards bloodletting and cupping[A] in the knowledge that this will procure him well-being, so the heart is inclined towards good and pious deeds if it knows that its felicity in the Hereafter is conditional upon them.

When [the heart] connects with the root of inclination by way of knowledge, inclination and perseverance will be required of it. For, perseverance in seeking and desiring the attributes of the heart through action is like sustenance and nourishment for these attributes—indeed the attribute is nurtured[4] and strengthened through perseverance. [For example], one's inclination to seek knowledge or leadership cannot but be weak at the outset. However, if one adheres to the demand of inclination and occupies himself with knowledge,[5] the cultivation of leadership and the actions demanded by these, his inclination is confirmed and takes root and he would be hard put to remove it.[6] Had he [from the start] opposed its demand, his inclination would have weakened and subsided, perhaps ceased and vanished.

For example, take someone who beholds a beautiful face and his natural inclination tends towards it a little. If he should follow what his inclination demands and thus persist in his gaze, exchange, company and conversation,[7] his inclination would be confirmed until it is no longer a matter of choice and he is unable to remove it. But if he weans himself from the start and opposes the requirement of inclination, it would be like depriving the attribute of inclination of sustenance and nourishment. It would be [like a] sharp and brusque slap to the face which causes [the

[A] Both are medical procedures.

inclination] to weaken and subside, and, [finally,] to be uprooted and expunged.

The same goes for all attributes and good and pious deeds. Through them one wishes for the Hereafter; through the vices one wishes for this world, not the Hereafter.[8] The soul's inclination towards otherworldly acts of goodness and its renunciation of this-worldly acts free it for the invocation and contemplation [of God]. But this is established only through perseverance in acts of piety,[9] and the abandonment of sinning through the limbs. This is because there is a relationship between the heart and the limbs and each is affected by the other. You will note that when a limb undergoes surgery, the heart feels pain. And again, when the heart is pained by its knowledge of a beloved's death, or assailed by something fearful, the limbs are affected, the whole body trembles and [one's] colour changes.

Now, the heart is the root to which [all is] subordinate. It is like the ruler or the shepherd; the limbs are like the servants, the flock or the subordinates. The limbs serve the heart by confirming the attributes in it. The heart is the goal, the members are the instruments leading to the goal. This is why the Prophet (may God bless him and grant him peace) said, 'The body contains a lump of flesh by grace of which, when it thrives, the rest of the body also thrives.' And he said, 'O God, make the shepherd and the flock prosper.'[10] By 'shepherd' he meant the heart. And God said, *It is neither their flesh nor their blood that reaches God, but the devoutness from you*[11]—this being the attribute of the heart.

From this perspective, there is no doubt that the acts of the heart are on the whole superior to the movements of the limbs. Hence, intention by necessity is superior to all [the acts], since it consists of the heart's inclination towards the good, its desire for it. For our purpose, the limbs' actions accustom the heart to desire the good and to establish the inclination towards [the good],[12] so as to be free of the worldly appetites and occupy itself with invocation and reflection. The good is necessarily so in relation to the purpose, because it resides in the goal itself.

It is like the stomach which, when it hurts, may be treated[13] either by ointment applied to the chest, or with drink and medicine that reach the stomach. Drink is better than ointment on the chest. The purpose of the ointment on the chest is that its effect should also reach the stomach. But that which has direct contact with the stomach is better and more useful.

This is how you ought to understand the effect of all pious acts—what is sought is solely to change the heart and to convert its attributes, and not [the attributes of] the limbs. Do not surmise that the purpose of placing the forehead on the ground is simply to join the forehead to the ground; rather it is to establish by virtue of habit the attribute of humility in the heart. If he who has humility in his heart humbles himself through his limbs[14] and in the form[A] of humility, then his humility becomes established. When he who finds tenderness in his heart for an orphan, strokes the orphan's head and kisses him, tenderness becomes established in his heart.[15]

This is why action without intention is useless—say, someone who strokes an orphan's head with an inattentive heart, thinking that he is stroking a garment: the effect cannot spread from his limbs to establish tenderness in his heart. Likewise, someone who prostrates himself [in prayer] inattentively, engrossed in worry about worldly things: the effect from his forehead placed on the ground will not spread to his heart to establish humility. Therefore, its presence is the same as its absence; and anything the presence or absence of which are equal, relative to the desired goal, is called 'void'.[B] Hence, it is said that worship without intention is void.[C] This is what is meant when a person acts inattentively. If his purpose is ostentation or the exaltation of another,

[A] Form or image. *Ṣūra* usually translates as form and refers to the *exterior* appearance of literally any 'thing' (*shay'*) into which one inquires.

[B] Meaning worthless or useless.

[C] Ibn Rushd notes that religious scholars generally agree on intention in acts of worship (*Bidāyat al-mujtahid* 6).

then the presence [of the act] is not equal to its absence. On the contrary, it increases its wickedness. He not only fails to establish the attribute desired and in the manner sought, but establishes an attribute one seeks to suppress—that of ostentation, a kind of inclination towards this world.

This is the purpose of [the prophetic saying] that the intention is better than the deed. In like manner are the words of the Prophet also understood, 'A good deed is in a writ decreed for the person who means to perform a good deed but does not.'[16] This is because the heart inclined towards the good, together with the shunning of passions and of love of this world. This is the purpose of good deeds, which the execution of the action establishes all the more.

Therefore, the purpose for shedding the blood of sacrifices is not the flesh and blood,[A] but the heart's inclination away from the love of this world and the giving freely out of preference for God Himself. This attribute occurs with the resolve and ardour of the intention, because if there is a hindering obstacle, then *it is neither their flesh nor their blood that reaches God, but the devoutness from you.*[B]

By devoutness (*taqwā*), here, I mean the heart. This is why the Prophet (may God bless him and grant him peace) said, 'There are in Medina a people who have joined with us in struggle'[C]—as mentioned earlier.[17] Their hearts were possessed of a true desire for the good; they gave freely of wealth and self, and aspired for martyrdom and the elevation of God's word—just like the hearts of those who departed for the holy war. They are separated bodily from the latter because of obstacles peculiar to causes that are

[A] This refers to the above quoted Qur'ānic verse: *It is neither their flesh nor their blood that reaches God, but the devoutness from you.*

[B] The hindering obstacle means an obstacle that hinders the actual performance of the sacrifice.

[C] 'There are many in Medina who, while still in the city, are joined with us in every valley we cross, every path we tread that vexes the unfaithful, every provision spent or hunger felt.'

external to the heart. But [actions] are sought only for establishing these [intended] attributes.

This is how, based on these interpretations, all the traditions we have presented in connection with the virtue of intention are to be taken. I have presented them in order to reveal to you their inner meanings, and we need not belabour [our point] with repetition.

CHAPTER FOUR

A Classification of How Actions are Related to Intention

KNOW THAT WHILE there are many kinds of actions—deed, utterance, movement, rest, attraction, repulsion, thought, remembrance, and an unimaginable, unexamined number of others still—they consist of three [main] categories: pious (*ṭāʿāt*), sinful (*maʿāṣī*), and permitted acts (*mubāḥāt*).[A]

THE FIRST CATEGORY: the sinful acts; these never change status with intention. Therefore, the ignoramus should not construe the Prophet's affirmation that 'action is through intention' differently by supposing that sin could somehow change into a pious deed through intention. One example is calumniating a person [just to please] another's heart; to feed a poor man with another's money; to build a school, mosque or hospice with ill-gained money—all the while aiming for what is good. This is all ignorance. Intention causes none of it to cease being inequity, violation and sin.

In fact, aiming for the good by means of a wrong and in opposition to the decree of religious law is an additional wrong. If [the person] is aware of this, then he is stubbornly resisting the law. If he does not know it, then his very ignorance is a wrong, since every Muslim is obliged to seek knowledge.[I] As for the good, it is the law that makes it good. How, then, could any wrong be good? Far be it, for it is hidden desire and secret passion which propagate this in the heart. If the heart inclines toward social standing in

[A] Though Ghazālī here lists pious acts first, he proceeds to define the sinful ones first.

order to win hearts and other personal gains,[2] then the devil will use this to deceive the ignorant.

This is why [Abū Muḥammad] Sahl [al-Tustarī] (may God be pleased with him) said, 'There is no greater sin against God (Exalted is He) than that of ignorance.' He was asked, 'O Abū Muḥammad, do you know of anything worse than ignorance?' 'Yea, the ignorance of ignorance,' he replied.[A3]

He said this because the ignorance of [one's] ignorance completely locks the door of learning. For how[4] can someone who bethinks himself completely knowledgeable learn? Hence, there is no better obedience to God than through knowledge. The summit of knowledge is knowledge of [what] knowledge is, just as the height of ignorance is the ignorance of [one's] ignorance.

Therefore, he who cannot tell useful from harmful knowledge preoccupies himself with the spurious sciences people rely on as a means to this world. This is the stuff of ignorance and the source of abasement for the learned.

What this means is that whoever intends the good through the wrong out of ignorance is not excused, unless he is still unpractised in Islam and has not yet had an opportunity to learn. God has said, *Ask the people who recollect, if ye know not.*[5] And, the Prophet said, 'The ignorant man is not excused his ignorance. And it is not licit for the ignorant to ignore his ignorance, nor for the learned to be silent with his knowledge.'[6]

The rulers curry favour by building mosques and schools with illicit money—just as do the pretenders to learnedness who impart knowledge to the insolent and the wicked; those given to dissolution and immorality; those whose only concern is to argue with the learned, spar with the foolish, sway people to their side and collect the vanities of this world; those who take the money of rulers, orphans and indigent alike. With [a little] learning these become the highway robbers along the path of God. Each one in his town is stirred to action for the Antichrist (*Dajjāl*), rushing

[A] As Makkī explains, this means being ignorant without knowing it.

upon the world, following passion, estranging himself from godliness and, by his example, emboldening people to sin against God. This knowledge then spreads to like-minded people, who wield it like an instrument and a means to [commit] wrong and follow passion—and so on down the chain. The evil consequences of all this are traceable to that person who taught him such a knowledge while aware of his reprobate intention and goal, and while seeing [in him] all manner of sins in utterances and deeds—in his eating, in his dress and in his abode. This learned person may die, but the effects of his wickedness spread throughout the world remain, say, for a thousand or two thousand years.

Fortunate is the person whose misdeeds die with him when he dies. The wonder is when he[A] utters, in his ignorance, 'Action is through intention', and I meant to spread the knowledge of religion through this.[B] It is he who used it iniquitously. The offence is his, not mine. My only purpose was that he use it well.' Now, the desire to lead and to have followers and the vainglory of towering knowledge put a gloss on [his actions] in his heart. The devil deceives him by means of the desire to lead. Would that I knew what he might say to a person who gives a highway robber a sword, together with a horse and the means of availing himself of his goal, and who says, 'I only wanted to be unstinting and generous, to [imitate] the beautiful attributes of God. I wanted him to fight with this sword and this horse in the way of God, since preparation of the mount and the military outpost[7] and the wherewithal to fight are among the best acts of piety. It is he who employed them for highway robbery. He is the sinner.'

Yet, the doctors of law agree by consensus that this is forbidden, even if generosity is the virtue which God loves best. Indeed, His Messenger said, 'To God belong three hundred attributes. He who draws closer to Him with but one shall enter Paradise, and

[A] That is, the learned.

[B] That is, through teaching the reprobate person.

generosity (*sakhā'*)[A] is the one He loves best.'[B] Why ever is this generosity forbidden, then? Should he not have noted the miscreant's juncture of circumstances? And if it appeared that the miscreant was accustomed to use weapons for mischief, then one should deny him his weapon, not offer him others.[8]

Knowledge is a weapon that the devil and God's foes use for fight. With it God's foes support passion. How can someone who always prefers his world to his religion, his passion to his afterlife, and who is powerless against these for lack of virtues, be permitted a kind of knowledge that assures him the fulfilment of his passions?

On the contrary, the learned of aforetime always took stock of the circumstances of those who came to them [for instruction]. When they noted that something was amiss in a supereregatory act,[C] they denied him and would not advance him. Whenever they noticed immorality from him, or the illicit rendered licit, they dissociated themselves from the person. They ejected him from their midst and refrained from speaking to him, let alone teaching him, because they knew that[9] anyone who learned something without acting upon it, but instead passed it over or did something else, sought nothing more than an instrument to commit wrong. The forefathers took refuge in God from the libertine who is knowledgeable in the *Sunna* [example of the Prophet] even more than the ignorant [libertine].[10]

A companion of Aḥmad b. Ḥanbal's related how he used to visit him for many years. Then it happened that Aḥmad turned away and dissociated himself from him. The man kept asking why this about-face. Aḥmad ignored him and then he said, 'I heard that you put up a mud wall touching the side of the walkway, and that you took a measure of the mud's thickness—the measure

[A] *Sakhā'* approaches 'munificence'. It is more than just generosity.

[B] There is an interesting discussion of this in Ibn ʿArabī's, *al-Futūḥāt al-makkiyyah* II:272.

[C] Supererogatory acts are voluntary, not mandatory acts of worship.

of a fingertip—from the Muslims' walkway. Therefore, you are not worthy to receive knowledge.'[11] This is how vigilant the forefathers were with respect to the circumstances of the seekers of knowledge.

This and similar things confound the foolish and those who follow the devil even if they wear a mantle[A] and wide sleeves and count among the loquacious and the verbose—I mean excessive in the sciences which contain neither caveat about this world nor stricture; which neither excite interest in the Hereafter nor invite to it. These are the sciences that pertain to created things and procure only the vanities of this world, the subservience of people and advantage over opponents.

Therefore, the Prophet's words 'action is through intention' are concerned, from among the three categories, with the pious and the permissible acts, to the exclusion of sinful ones. This is because a pious act can, through intent,[12] convert into a sinful act, just as the permissible can convert into either a sinful or a pious act by way of intent. However, the sin essentially can never change into a pious act by intent. Intention certainly has a bearing on it, but only when bad[13] intentions are linked to it,[B] where the burden doubles along with the magnitude of its evil consequences—as we mentioned in the *Book of Forgiveness*.[14]

THE SECOND CATEGORY: pious acts. These are connected to intentions through their root soundness and their manifold benefits. The 'root' is that one intends by [these acts] to worship God, nothing else. When the intention is dissimulation,[C] [the pious acts] become sins. As for the 'benefits', they become manifold when good intentions are abundant. Thus a single act of piety

[A] *Taylasān* is a shawl-like garment worn over the head and shoulders (Dozy, *Dictionnaire détaillé des noms des vêtements*, s. 278ff). This and the wide sleeves typify the dress of learned males.

[B] That is, when bad intentions are added to a sinful act.

[C] *Riyā'* (dissimulation or hypocrisy) suggests a good deed intended for show, not for God.

may intend many good things, and with every intention is a reward because each one is a good act. Every good act begets ten like it, as the report goes.[15]

An example of this is sojourning at the mosque, which is a pious act, though the person may intend several things by it until he achieves the virtuous actions of the godfearing, thereby attaining the levels of those who are close to God.[16] [Now] the *first*[A] consists in affirming that this is the house of God and that one enters [the mosque] as God's guest with the purpose of visiting his Lord in anticipation of what the Messenger of God (may God bless him and grant him peace) promised when he said, 'He who sojourns at the mosque surely visits God (Exalted is He); and the one visited is obliged to honour his visitor.'[17]

The *second* [intention] is when [the worshipper] awaits [the next] prayer after having prayed and thus [may be said to] remain in prayer the length of his wait.[18] This is what is meant by, *Stand fast* (wa-rābitū)![19]

The *third* is self-denial[B] by abstaining (*kaff*) from hearing and seeing and the [movement of the] limbs—[all] comings and goings. Isolating oneself[C] is abstaining (*kaff*), as in fasting, which is a form of self-denial. This is why the Messenger of God said, 'Monasticism for my community is sojourning in the mosques.'[20]

The *fourth* is applying oneself to the concentration upon God; the necessity to reflect on the Hereafter from the inner self (*sirr*); and the eschewing of every preoccupation that detracts from Him by retreating to the mosque.

The *fifth* is to be devoted exclusively to the remembrance of

[A] By *first*, Ghazali means the first of the intentions of the one action of sojourning at a mosque.

[B] We have translated *tarahhub* as self-denial, but it literally means 'to become a monk'. Ghazālī is linking this intention to the *ḥadīth* that follows on monasticism (*rahbāniyya*). *Tarahhub* and *rahbāniyya* have the same radical, *r-h-b*.

[C] There is a long tradition in Islam of isolating oneself (*iʿtikāf*) in a mosque for the sake of concentrated worship. This is in imitation of the Prophet who used to practice *iʿtikāf* especially during the final days of the month of Ramadan.

God or listening to remembrance or reminding others of Him. As the report says, 'He who goes to the mosque in the morning to remember God (Exalted is He) or reminding others of Him is as the fighter in the way of God (Exalted is He).'[21]

The *sixth* is to have in mind the benefit of learning by enjoining the good and prohibiting the evil.[A22] For the mosque hardly lacks those who badly perform their ritual prayers or who engage in what is not licit. Therefore, he should enjoin what is good and guide [others] to religion, that he may share in what good is learns from it, and that his own good deeds be multiplied.

The *seventh* is gaining a brother[B] in [the path of] God (*akh fī Allāh*). Indeed, this is 'booty and treasure' to the abode of the Hereafter.[23] For the mosque is a sanctuary for the people of religion who love God and love each other in God.

The *eighth* is renouncing sins in deference to God and being too ashamed[24] to abuse the sanctity of the house of God. Al-Ḥasan b. ʿAlī (may God be pleased with both of them) said, 'For someone given to frequenting the mosque, God's reward is one of seven traits: the gain of a brother in God; a blessing sent down; a refined knowledge; a word that leads[25] to guidance; his shunning of what is base; abandonment of offences from fear; doing so in deference.'[26]

This is the path of multiple intentions and by it you must measure all other pious and permitted acts. For there is no pious act that does not carry several intentions. However, they become present in the heart of the believing servant of God only insofar

[A] This injunction is considered the key collective duty of all Muslims.

[B] That is, a *spiritual* brother. The generic term 'brother' in Islam as elsewhere includes 'sister'. One must keep in mind, here as elsewhere, that words like 'brother' are not semantically sex- but *gender*-specific (i.e., taken in the proper grammatical sense). It is the same with personal pronouns, unless of course the context itself points to either a man or a woman. The modern concern with the social semantics of 'gender' is completely foreign to the premodern authors because it was the accepted rules of grammar (not ideological or cultural issues) that governed their utterances.

as he earnestly seeks the good, pondering it and embarking upon. This is how actions are kept pure and the benefits multiplied.

THE THIRD CATEGORY: permitted acts. There is no permitted act through which nearness [to God] is achieved and the highest levels are attained which is not subject to intention or [several] intentions. For who is a greater loser than the one who neglects [intention] and who ventures forth in the manner of dumb beasts, heedless and carefree? The servant of God should not disdain a passing thought, step or moment.[27] All this will be asked about on the Day of Resurrection: Why did he act thus? What was his purpose? And this, for permitted acts, untarnished[28] by anything prohibited. This is why the Messenger said, 'To things legal, a [final] reckoning; and to things illegal, a punishment.'[29] In a tradition narrated by Muʿādh b. Jabal, the Prophet says, 'The servant of God shall be asked about everything, including the kohl around his eyes, the tads of earth on his two fingers and the feel of his brother's garb.'[30] And in another tradition, 'He who perfumes himself for God (Exalted is He) shall on the Day of Resurrection go forth with a scent more fragrant than that of musk. He who perfumes himself for any other than God (Exalted is He) shall on the Day of Resurrection go forth with an odour more putrid than carrion.'[31] The use of perfume is permitted, but it must have an intention.

You may ask, 'How could perfume be intended when it is [a pleasure] allotted to the self? And, how can one perfume oneself for God?'

Know that he who perfumes himself, say, on a Friday and on other occasions, may intend merely to enjoy the pleasures of this world. Or, his intention may be to boast openly of his plentiful money, to the envy[32] of his peers; to show off before people in order to raise his standing in their hearts and to be remembered by his pleasant fragrance; or to endear himself to the hearts of strange women, if he is permitted a glance at them; and for countless other reasons. All this makes perfuming sinful and he will thereby be more putrid than carrion at the Resurrection.

The exception is the first intention, taking pleasure and enjoyment—this is not sinful. However, one will be asked about it, and he whose account is contested will incur punishment.[33] But he who acquires something permitted of this world will not suffer on account of it in the Hereafter. He will only lack the ease of the Hereafter by the same measure. Suffice it to say that he loses because he hastens towards what is perishable and misses out on the imperishable.

As for good intentions [in the use of perfume], they consist of the intention to observe the tradition of God's Messenger on Friday and, thereby, the intention to honour the mosque and to show respect for God's house. He does not consider it fit to enter it as a guest of God without being well-perfumed,[34] his aim here being pleasantness for his neighbours inside the mosque, that they may find ease beside him with the enjoyment of his perfume. Hence, his aim is to remove the disagreeable odours emanating from him which disturb the humours. He aims to shut the door of calumny to the vilifiers who calumniate about disagreeable odours, and because of that are disobedient to God. Someone subjected to calumny while capable of safeguarding against it shares in the offence—as is said:

> If from people you make to depart
> And they your leave resolve to deny,
> then 'tis they, surely, who depart

Said God, *Revile not those [idols] upon which they call besides God, lest they out of spite and in their ignorance revile God.*[35] By this He indicated that whatever gives rise to evil is itself evil.

[Another good intention for the use of perfume has to do] with the aim to attend to the head in order to raise one's astuteness and intelligence, facilitating the discernment of the principals of one's religion through thinking. Shāfiʿī said, 'He who sweetens his scent, will increase in mind.'

A person of discernment is not incapable of this and similar intentions, if the exchange for the Hereafter and the search for the good predominate in his heart. If nothing more than worldly ease prevails in his heart, these [correct] intentions will not occur to him. And, if he is reminded of them, he will remain unmoved. His share of them is nothing but mental chatter and this can hardly be considered an intention.

Permitted things being numerous, the intentions cannot be enumerated. Thus, make the one [example of perfume above] the measure for others. This is why a knowledgeable person from aforetime said, 'I prefer to have an intention for everything—my food, drink, sleep, entering of the lavatory.'[36] All this enables one to draw close to God (Exalted is He), since any means that preserves the body and frees the heart of the body's requirements is an aid to religion. He who intends by eating to protect his acts of worship and by physical union to fortify his religion, to gratify his family's hearts,[37] and to beget a righteous child who worships God after him, and through him to increase the community of Muḥammad, he is obedient in both food and marriage.

As the most prevalent of the self's pleasures are eating and wedlock,[38] aiming [to do] the good through them is permissible for the person whose heart is fastened predominantly upon the Hereafter. This is why[39] he should keep his intention good, irrespective of how much wealth he may lose, saying, 'It is in the way of God.' If he learns that another person has slandered him,[40] let his heart be at ease [with the thought] that he [the slanderer] shall carry his sins and [the slanderer's] good deeds will be transferred to his registry. Let him intend this by refraining from giving reply. For according to the report, 'The servant of God shall be taken to account, and his actions invalidated because the baneful has impinged upon them, whereupon he will deserve the Fire. Then, shall be announced to him those of his righteous deeds by which he will deserve Paradise. And he shall marvel and say, "O Lord, these are deeds I have never performed." And it shall be said to him, "These are the deeds by which you were slandered, harmed and wronged."'[41]

According to another report, 'The servant of God shall appear on the Day of Resurrection with good deeds akin to mountains—if they are granted to him, he shall enter Paradise. But he had wronged so-and-so, execrated that person, struck this person. Therefore, his good deeds will decrease for this and decrease for that, until no good deed remains for him. The angels will say that his good deeds have been exhausted and yet seekers [of redress] still remain. God will say, "Allocate to him their sins and strike a path for him to the Fire."'[42]

In sum, beware, but beware of disdaining any of your actions—you are never safe from their deceptions and calamities. Do not count on justifying them on the Day of Questioning and Account. For God (Exalted is He) is well-informed about you and sees—*he utters not a word but there is a sentinel by him, ready [to inscribe it]*.[43]

One of the forefathers said, 'I wrote a letter and wanted to dry [the ink] on my neighbour's wall, but I was reluctant. Then I said, "Dust, what is dust?" And I dusted it over.[44] Then I heard a voice say to me, "He who thinks little of dust will soon learn what he will receive in bad account."'[45]

A man was once praying with [Sufyān] al-Thawrī and saw that he had his garment inside out. He apprised him of this. The latter stretched out his hand to put the garment aright but stopped short. The man asked him about this. [Sufyān] answered, 'I wore it for God (Exalted is He) and have no wish to tidy it for anyone else.'[46]

Said al-Ḥasan [al-Baṣrī], 'One man will grab hold of another on the Day of Resurrection and say, "God stands between you and me."[A] [The other man] will say, "By God, I know ye not." The other will say, "But you took a brick from my wall, and you took a thread from my garment."'[47]

This and similar reports pierce the hearts of the fearful. If you are among those in a position of authority[B], and are not deluded, then you must observe yourself and make yourself strictly

[A] In other words, God is our witness.

[B] Literally, if you are among those who can determine and deny (*ulū'l-ʿazm wa'l-nahy*).

accountable before the final accounting bears upon you. Examine your circumstances. And neither remain at rest nor make a move without first pondering why you are moving; what your intention is; what it procures for you from this world; what you may miss in the Hereafter; and how you give this world preponderance over the Hereafter. If you find that religion is the only motive, then firm up your resolve and what thought [you entertain]. Else, desist! But examine also your heart when you desist or refrain [from something]. For refraining from acting is itself an act, and must have sound intention. Therefore, the motive[48] should not be a hidden, inscrutable passion. Let neither the appearances of things nor acknowledged good deeds mislead you, but fathom what lies deep and concealed and you will then dissociate yourself from the circle of the deluded.[49]

It is related that Zachariah (peace be upon him) was repairing a wall with mud. He had been hired by certain people who had given him a loaf of bread,[50] since he ate only from what he earned. Some people came to him; he did not invite them to eat and finished [his meal]. They were astonished by him, knowing of his liberality and abstinence, and because they assumed that it is good to share food. He said, 'A people hired me to work, bringing me the bread for strength while I work for them. If you eat with me, neither you nor I will have enough, and I shall weaken while working for them.'[51]

Thus, the discerning person sees the things hidden with the light of God. [Zachariah's] weakness in work would have been a dereliction of duty, [while] refraining from sharing food is a failure of graciousness. And meritorious acts (*faḍā'il*) are not judged like duties (*farā'id*).

A man said, 'I went to Sufyān [al-Thaqafī][52] while he ate. He did not speak to me until he had licked his fingers. Then he said, "If I had not taken [this meal] by religious [duty], I would have wished you to eat from it."'[53]

Said Sufyān [al-Thawrī], 'He who invites another to his meal while [the guest] has no desire to eat of it, and the latter accedes and eats—he has committed two offences. If the man does not eat, his is a single offence.'[54] By the one offence, [Sufyān] meant hypocrisy; by the other, that he should expose his brother to something he would resent if he knew of it.[A]

This is how the servant [of God] ought to inspect his intention in every act. He must neither proceed nor retreat save with an intention. If he has no intention, therefore, he must pause; for, [having] intention is not a matter of choice.[B]

[A] In the sense that his friend would be offended if he found out that the invitation was not sincere.

[B] That is, one cannot choose not to have an intention. Every action must have an intention.

CHAPTER FIVE

An Exposition on that Intention is Not a Matter of Choice

KNOW THAT THE ignorant person hears our advice on refining and multiplying the intention, together with the words of the Prophet, 'Works are through intention', and then says to himself when he teaches, engages in commerce or eats, 'I intended to teach for God, do commerce for God or eat for God.' And he takes this for an intention. Far from it! This is just an inner discourse, a discourse of the tongue and of mere thought,[1] or the succession from one notion to another. Intention is far removed from all this.[2]

Intention is the soul's motivation, orientation and inclination towards what appears to it to contain a purpose in this world or the next. When there is no inclination, it is impossible to contrive or to acquire one by sheer will. That would be like a satiated person saying, 'I intended to crave and be favourably disposed to food'; or, an indifferent person saying, 'I intend to love so-and-so—to value and have high regard for him in my heart.' This is inconceivable. Indeed, the only way to bring the heart to turn, be inclined or be oriented towards anything would be by securing the means[A] for it; and this, [depends] on whether one is capable or incapable of it.

Rather, the soul is motivated to act in response to the aim that motivates and agrees with it. As long as the person is not convinced that his aim depends on a certain deed, he will not tend in the direction of [that deed] considering that he is incapable of

[A] *Asbāb*—lit., 'causes'.

being convinced at every moment. But when the person is [convinced], his heart has orientation so long as it is free and uncommitted to [another] active aim that is stronger than the [first]. This is not always the case. There are many ways in which motives and commitments come into play. They differ according to person, circumstances and deeds.

For example, if the appetite for physical union preponderates in the absence of any religious or worldly conviction that the purpose is to have a child, one could not engage in amorous relations with the intention of having a child. On the contrary, this is possible only with the intention to suppress the appetite, the intention being a response to the motive. However, [here] there is no motive but the appetite; therefore, how could one intend a child?

He who is not convinced in his heart that upholding the custom of wedlock, in imitation of the Messenger of God (may God bless him and grant him peace), augments its virtue,[3] cannot possibly intend to marry following the example of the Prophet. He may say so with his tongue and heart; however, that would be mere talk and not intention.

The best way to acquire this intention consists, for instance, in firstly strengthening one's faith through the injunctions of religion;[4] [then] in strengthening one's faith in the greatness of the reward for striving to increase the community of Muḥammad (may God bless him and grant him peace); and in shunning whatever draws one back from [having] offspring because of it being a weighty burden, lengthy toil, and so on. When a person does this, the desire to have a child for the reward may be incited in his heart. This desire moves him and sets his limbs in motion for fulfilment of the marriage contract. If the power moving [the limbs] rouses the tongue to accept the contract according to this dominant motive of the heart, the person has intention. If this is not the case, then what he himself thinks and repeats to himself about the purpose of having a child is mere imaginings and drivel.

This is why[5] some forefathers refrained from certain pious deeds in the absence of intention. They used to say, 'In this we had no intention.' So much so, Ibn Sīrīn[A] did not pray at the funeral of al-Ḥasan al-Baṣrī, saying, 'I lack the intention.'[6]

One man arranging his hair called out to his wife to bring him a comb. She replied, 'Shall I bring the mirror?' He fell silent a spell, then said, 'Yes.' When asked about [his silence], he said, 'My intention was for the comb, not the mirror; therefore, I paused for God to provide [the intention].'[7]

When Ḥammād b. Abī Sulaymān,[8] one of the most celebrated scholars of Kufa, died, Thawrī was asked, 'Shall you not attend his funeral?' He replied, 'Had I an intention, I would.'[9]

And when a goodly act was asked of one of them, he used to say, 'If God (Exalted is He) bestows an intention upon me, I shall act on it.'[10]

Ṭā'ūs [b. Kaysān al-Yamānī] never spoke without intention. When asked to speak, he did not; and he began to speak when he was not asked. He was queried about this and said, 'Would you prefer that I speak without intention? When I have an intention, I act on it.'[11]

It is said that when Dā'ūd b. al-Muḥabbar had composed his *Book of the Intellect*,[12] Aḥmad b. Ḥanbal went to ask him for it. Aḥmad leafed through the book and returned it. 'What is the matter?' asked Dā'ūd. Aḥmad replied, 'It contains weak chains of transmission.' 'I did not compose based on chains of transmission. Look at the matter itself. Looking at it through the work itself will benefit you.'[13] Said Aḥmad, 'Return it to me, then, that I may look at it from your viewpoint.' He took it and kept it long with him. Finally, he said, 'God bless you for it! I benefited from it.'[14]

Ṭā'ūs was requested to make supplications [to God], to which request he replied, 'When I find the intention.'[15]

One man said, 'For a month I have been seeking the intention to visit an [ailing] man, but have not found it in me.'[16]

Said ʿĪsā b. Kathīr [al-Asadī], 'I was walking along with Maymūn b. Mahrān. At the door of his house, I turned away. But

[A] His father was a *mawlā* of Anas b. Mālik (d. 91–93/709–711).

his son asked him, "Will you not offer him supper?" "It is not my intention," said he'.[17] This is because intention follows the viewpoint (*naẓar*).[A] Therefore, as the viewpoint changes so changes the intention.

[The forefathers] did not believe in executing any action without intention because they knew that intention is the spirit of action.[B] Action without a true intention is show and pretence; it is a cause for rejection, not closeness [to God]. They knew that intention does not consist in merely uttering 'I intend' with the tongue.[18] Rather, it is an incentive of the heart which occurs in the manner of inspiration[C] from God (Exalted is He). At times it is easy, at times difficult.

Granted, the intention [to perform] good deeds is, in most instances, more easily secured by someone whose heart is dominated by the affairs of religion. If his heart generally inclines towards the source of goodness, he will be motivated in the main towards the particulars [of goodness]. But this is not easy for someone whose heart inclines towards this world and is dominated by it. Indeed, he cannot fulfil [his religious] duties without considerable effort. His goal should be to remember the Fire and to beware of its punishment, or [to remember] the comfort of Paradise and awaken in himself the desire for it. Perhaps then a weak motive will rise up in him;[19] his reward will be in proportion to his desire and intention.

Now, obedience [to God] based on the intention to exalt God by virtue of His right to obedience and servantship is not easy[20] for someone who desires this world. It is the rarest and highest of intentions, and he is rare on the face of the earth who understands it, much less puts it into practice.[21]

[A] Namely, how you view something.

[B] *Rūḥ al-ʿamal*, in the sense of source or cause.

[C] *Futūḥ* (sing., *fatḥ*) has been translated here as inspiration; its literal meaning is 'opening', and in the language of Sufism it often signifies spiritual realisation or illumination.

People's intentions in good deeds fall into [various] categories. One person acts out of a motivation of fear because he is wary of the Fire. Another acts out of a motivation of hope and this is the desire for Paradise. When this takes place relative to the aim of obeying God and extolling Him and nothing else, it may be counted among the correct intentions, as it is an inclination towards what is promised in the Hereafter, even if it is of a kind familiar in this world.[A] [Sexual] relief and [satisfying] the stomach are the dominant motives [in human beings], although their ultimate fulfilment is in Paradise. Therefore, he who acts for the sake of Paradise acts only [to satisfy] his stomach and sexual urge; he is like a bad hireling. His is the rank of feeble-mindedness. He will attain to it [Paradise] through his deeds, for most of the people of Paradise are feeble of mind (*bulh*).

On the other hand, the worship of the people of insight (*dhawī al-albāb*) does not forgo[22] the remembrance of God and thinking about Him out of love of His beauty and majesty. The remainder of [their] acts are confirmations and consequences [of this]. These

[A] The scriptures of Islam (both the revealed Qur'ān and the utterings of the Prophet himself) describe the Hereafter in *human* language, naturally for the comprehension of *all* human beings; hence the imagery of food, companionship, etc. Too literalist an interpretation may have the unintended consequence of implying that we can know, as we stand within bounds of *this* world, what God purposely leaves hidden about the Afterlife—that is, beyond what human beings learn and inherit through the prophethood of Muḥammad. From a worldly viewpoint, one cannot see the Afterlife except what God reveals of it at the station of prophethood through Muḥammad. But this is an affirmation of the *reality* of the Afterlife, which Ghazali of course accepts, not just idle speculation about the unseen. It does not contradict resurrection after death, but on the contrary, reaffirms it. But we easily forget that 'death', in Islam and other scriptural traditions, is final and can *only* be qualified with finality. Short of this, religion can easily degenerate into childish notions about killing and dying and about God then sorting out everything 'later'. The Afterlife cannot be just another room in the same house. There is an ethical dimension to teachings about the Afterlife which is as easily lost in literalist interpretations as it is in speculative ones.

[people] rise above any inclination toward the object of amorous union and the nourishments of Paradise; they do not seek them. Rather, they are the ones who *call on God day and night, desiring only His countenance.*[23] People are rewarded according to their intentions. Surely, they will luxuriate in the sight of His noble countenance. They will scoff at those who turn to face[A] the 'wide-eyed companions' (*ḥūr al-ʿayn*);[B24] just as those who luxuriate[25] in the sight of the 'wide-eyed companions' scoff at those who luxuriate when they face figures fashioned from clay[C]—albeit more. For, the difference between the beauty of the Presence of Lordship (*ḥaḍrat al-rubūbiyya*) and the beauty of the 'wide-eyed companions' is far greater than the difference between the beauty of the 'wide-eyed companions' and [that of] figures fashioned from clay.

The high importance that the animal-passionate souls[D] place upon getting their wish, such as mixing with beautiful women,

[A] *Wajh* (face) is in the singular.

[B] 'Wide-eyed' in the sense of having an intense gaze upon the believer in Paradise. *Ḥūr al-ʿayn* (or the houris) is taken from the Qur'ān (XLIV.54, LII.20, LV.72, LVI.22), where they are clearly regarded as the believers' intimate *companions* in Paradise. In his commentary on the Qur'ān, *Anwār al-tanzīl wa asrār al-ta'wīl* (p. 659), Bayḍāwī alludes to the pointless debate surrounding their nature, part of the controversy referring to whether or not they are like the women of this world. In his view, nothing about their location or time can be said. The resurrected are simply said to join to the houris, who 'bring fruits' to the them and 'fill their every desire'. Bayḍāwī also explains that the houris praise God continually from the depth of their consciousness of the Hereafter and of death. Although they are referred to in the feminine form, in a grammatical sense, their 'sex' can only be conditional on that of the servant. Paradise is 'where' God rewards his servants, fulfils His promise, and grants greater felicity than any earthly pleasure. Heaven symbolizes the fulfilment of what God has ordained *may not* be completely fulfilled on earth. We exist on earth, on the other hand, by virtue of our physical limitations.

[C] That is, human beings, which appears to answer Bayḍāwī's sceptical view of the idea that houris are like earthly women.

[D] 'Animal-passionate' refers to the lower faculties within the same human 'soul' and which we share with all other animals.

while turning away from the beauty of God's noble countenance,[26] is like a beetle giving high appraisal of its mate and confidante but refraining from beholding the beauty of women's faces. Hence, the blindness of most hearts to the vision of God's beauty and majesty resembles the beetle's blindness, [which prevents it] from perceiving the beauty of women—which beauty it[27] never detects or notices. If the beetle had an intellect and were told about women, it would still think lightly of those who turn to [the women]. *But they will not cease to dispute*;[28] *over what they delight in possessing*;[29] *and for this did He create them.*[30]

It is narrated that Aḥmad b. Khiḍrawayh [al-Balkhī] saw his Lord in a dream. His Lord said to him, 'Everyone asks Paradise of Me, save Abū Yazīd [al-Bisṭāmī], who asks for Me.'[31]

Seeing[32] his Lord in a dream, Abū Yazīd said, 'O Lord, what is the way to Thee?' His Lord replied, 'Abandon yourself and come to Me.'[33]

After he died, [Abū Bakr] al-Shiblī was seen in a dream and asked, 'What has God done with you?' He said, 'He does not call me to task for claims based on proof,[A] except for a single utterance. I once said, "What loss is greater than the loss of Paradise?" "Nay, what loss is greater than failing to meet Me?" said He.'[34]

The point is that the intentions [described] above differ in degrees. When one of these intentions prevails in a person's heart, perhaps he will not revile[35] forgoing another. Knowing these realities may give rise to actions and deeds which the literalists among the jurists will deny. We hold that he who intends [to carry out] a legally permitted act (*mubāḥ*), but not an act of virtue, the legally permitted act is primary and the virtuous act is transferred to it.[B36] In his case, the virtuous act [alone] is insufficient, because actions are performed through intentions.[C]

[A] *Daʿāwī* are empty or false claims.

[B] 'Transferred to it' means that the permitted act becomes a meritorious act too.

[C] Meaning: and there was no intention here to commit a virtuous act.

An example of this is forgiveness, which is superior to [simply] triumphing when wronged. There may be an intention to triumph without forgiveness, in which case [the former] would be more correct. It is the same when a person intends to eat, drink and sleep in order to give himself rest and strength[37] for future acts of worship. His intention here is neither to fast nor to pray. For him eating and sleeping are better. Should he tire from devotions, because he is too assiduous, and his enthusiasm subsides and his desire weakens—knowing that if he took an hour's rest in amusement and conversation his alacrity might return—then amusement is better for him than prayer.

Said Abū Dardā', 'I give myself rest with something amusing. This is a support for me [in doing] what is right.'[38]

Said ʿAlī (may God ennoble his countenance), 'Give your hearts rest—for if they are forced to loathe, they become blind.'[39]

These are subtleties which only the adroit among the learned, not the narrowly literal traditionist,[A] can understand. Indeed, someone skilled in medicine may treat the feverish with meat despite the latter's high temperature; whereas someone inexperienced in medicine will not consider this. In this, the former hopes first [to allow the patient] to regain his strength in order to bear treatment with a curative. Similarly, the person skilled in the game of chess will freely give up his rook or knight in order to win. A man of limited insight (*ḍaʿīf al-baṣīra*) will laugh at him in sheer astonishment. Likewise, a clever fighter escapes his opponent's front and goes to the latter's rear as a ruse to draw him into a tight position, and then attacks or overpowers him.

This is the approach to the path of God. All of it is battling the devil and ministering to the heart. Someone of insight (*baṣīr*) who is accomplished [with God's support[B]] pauses[C] for subtle ruses

[A] The term *ḥashwiyya* usually refers to anyone who insists on pure formality or on pseudo-religious banalities without much understanding.

[B] In this context, *tawfīq* signifies the support of God.

[C] That is, in the path of God.

along [the way] which the weak-minded dismiss. Therefore, the disciple ought not to shrink back in denial of what he sees from his master; nor should the pupil contradict his teacher. He ought to recognise the limit of his own insight. What he cannot understand of [the master's and teacher's] states he should leave with them until the secrets of these [states] are unveiled to him, having reached their rank and level. And from God is the best of success.

PART II

ON SINCERITY, ITS MERIT, REALITY AND DEGREES

CHAPTER SIX

An Exposition of the Merit of Sincerity

GOD (EXALTED IS HE) said, *And they have been commanded only to worship God, their devotion to Him sincere…*;[1] *Is sincere religion not God's due?*;[2] *Except those who repent, make amends, adhere to God and purify their religion*;[3] *Whoever expects to meet his Lord, let him act righteously and in his worship associate nothing with his Lord*[4]—[all] were revealed about the one who acts for God and loves to offer Him praises.

The Prophet said, 'There are three things about which the heart of a Muslim man is uninhibited: sincerity (*ikhlāṣ*) of the action [performed] for God…'[5]

Musʿab b. Saʿd [al-Madanī] related that his father [Ibn Abī al-Waqqāṣ] believed he had an advantage over other Companions of the Prophet. The Prophet (may God bless him and grant him peace) said, 'God Almighty and Majestic helps this community through its weak, and through their supplications, their sincerity and their prayers.'

On the authority of al-Ḥasan [al-Baṣrī], the Messenger of God said, 'God (Exalted is He) says, "Sincerity is one of My secrets, which I consign to the heart of the servant I love."'[6]

Said ʿAlī b. Abī Ṭālib, 'Do not worry about the scarcity of actions but about their acceptance. For the Prophet told Muʿādh b. Jabal, "Make your action pure (*akhliṣ*) and only a little of it shall suffice."'[7]

Said the Prophet, 'No servant acts sincerely for God for forty days for whom the wellsprings of wisdom shall not issue forth from his heart to his tongue.'[8]

And he said, 'On the Day of Resurrection, three shall be questioned first: A man upon whom God had bestowed knowledge. Of him He will ask him, "What have you done with what you have learned?" His answer shall be, "Lord, I have set myself to it day and night." But God (Exalted is He) will say, "You lie." And the angels will say, "You lie—nay, you wished it be said, 'So-and-so is learned.' And was it not so said?" And a man upon whom God had bestowed money. God will ask him, "I have lavished thee—how have you carried yourself?" The man will say, "Lord, I have given in alms day and night." "You lie," God will say. And the angels, "You lie—nay, you wished it be said, 'So-and-so is generous.' And was it not so said?" And to a man who was killed in the path of God, God (Exalted is He) will say, "How have you carried yourself?" "Lord, I was commanded to fight, and so I made battle until I was slain." "You lie," will God say. And the angels, "You lie—nay, you wish it be said, 'So-and-so is brave.' And was it not so said?"'[9]

Abū Hurayra said, 'Then God's Messenger (may God bless him and grant him peace) patted me on the thigh and said, "Abū Huraryra, these are the first people with whom hell, on the Day of Resurrection, is lit afire."'

When he who transmitted this tradition went to Muʿāwiya and recounted it, Muʿāwiya wept until he almost expired. He then said, *Those who desire the life of this world and its glitter...*—thus spoke God.'[A]

In one of the Israelite tales, a man had been performing devotions to God for a long spell. Some people came to tell him about a people who worshipped a tree in God's stead. This brought him to anger. Resting his axe on his shoulder, he went to cut down the tree. But Iblīs[B] greeted him in the shape of an elderly man, 'Where to, God have mercy on you?'

[A] *Those who desire the life of this world and its glitter—We shall requite them for their deeds therein without diminution* (Q. XI.15).

[B] Iblīs is the Qur'ānic name for Satan.

'I want to cut this tree,' the man replied.

He said to him, 'What is it to you...abandoning your devotions and self-preoccupations for something else.'

'This is part of my worship,' said the man.

'I shan't let you cut it down.' Whereupon he fought the man. But the latter flung Iblīs to the ground and sat upon his breast.

Iblīs muttered to him, 'Release me that I may speak to thee.' The man got off him and Iblīs said to him, 'Man, God (Exalted is He) has relieved thee of this. 'Tis no duty of yours—ye worship it not. Nor are you responsible for anyone else! It is God who sends prophets to every clime on earth. Had He wished it, He would have sent them to the owners of [this tree] and ordered them to cut it down.'

'I must cut it,' said the man. Iblīs drove upon him [again] for a fight. But the man overpowered him, brought him down and sat himself upon his breast.

Powerless, Iblīs said to him, 'Would you like to know what separates you and me,[10] and what is better for you and more beneficial?'

'And what is that?'

'Release me that I may tell thee.' This he did. Then Iblīs said, 'You are but a poor fellow, with nothing to your name. You rely on people to provide you with everything. Perhaps you wish to rise above your brethren and to lavish your neighbour; to be sated[11] and independent of people.'

'Yes.'

'So withdraw from this affair, and I shall take it upon me every night to place beside your head two *dinars*. When you rise, you will take them to spend on yourself and your children, and to give alms to your brethren. This is better for you and for the Muslims than cutting the tree, in place of which another will be planted.[12] Cutting it will neither harm nor benefit the believers.'

The man pondered these words, 'The old man is right. I am no prophet that I must cut down the tree. God has not commanded me to cut it that I would disobey Him if I did not—what he said to me is more profitable.'[13]

The man promised to fulfil this, and swore to it. He returned to his place of worship and stayed overnight. When he woke in the morning, he saw two *dinars* near his head. He took them. The same thing happened the next day. The third morning and thereafter, however, he found nothing. Angered, he rested his axe on his shoulder.

Iblīs greeted him in the form of an old man, 'Where to?'

'To cut that tree!' said the man.

'You lied, by God! You cannot do this…and *must* not do it.' The man made for Iblīs bent on doing to him what he had done the first time, 'How wrong you are!'

But Iblīs took hold of him and wrestled him down. The man was like a sparrow about his legs. Iblīs sat upon his breast and said, 'Turn away from this matter or I will surely slay thee.'

The man looked and saw he could not overcome him. 'You have beaten me. Now let go and tell me how,' he implored, 'first I overpowered you, and now you overpower me.'

Iblīs said, 'Because the first time you were angry for God. Your intention was the Hereafter, and so God let you subjugate me. This time you were angry for yourself and this world, and I overpower you.'[14]

This story reaffirms God's words *…except those of Thy servants who are sincere among them.*[15] For only through sincerity will the man be delivered from the devil.

This is why Maᶜrūf al-Karkhī used to strike himself and say, 'O my self, be sincere and you shall find deliverance.'

Said Yaᶜqūb al-Makfūf, 'The sincere person is one who can suppress his good as well as his bad deeds.'

Said Abū Sulaymān [al-Dārānī],[16] 'Fortunate is the person who takes but a single sound step by which he desires nothing but God (Exalted is He).'[17]

ᶜUmar b. al-Khaṭṭāb wrote to Abū Mūsā al-Ashᶜarī, 'For the person whose intention is sincere, it is enough that God's offering to him be what people give him.'[18]

Chapter Six

Said one of the Friends of God[A] to a brother of his, 'Make sincere the intention in your actions and less action will suffice for you.'[19]

Said Ayyūb [b. Abī Taymiyya] Sikhtiyānī, 'Making sincere the intentions of the acts is more consequential for them than all the acts.'[20]

Muṭarrif [b. ʿAbd Allāh b. al-Shikhkhīr] used to say, 'For him who purifies [things] are purified for him; for him who sullies [things] are sullied.'[21]

One man was seen in a dream [after he had died] and asked, 'How did you find your actions?' He replied, 'I found everything I did for God, down to the pomegranate seed I plucked from the path and even the she-cat which had died with us—I found [all] on the side of [my] good works. In my hood there had been a silk thread, which I found on the side of bad works.[B] For a donkey of mine that expired, worth a hundred *dinars*, I found no compensation, so I said, "The death of the cat [falls] within good works, but that of the donkey does not." But I was told that [the donkey] went wherever it was sent, but when I was apprised of its death I had said, "A curse from God"—and so my reward was lost. Had I said "In the way of God", I would have found it among my good works.'[22]

In another story, someone said, 'I used to give alms before people whose looks upon me pleased me. I found this neither a gain nor a liability.' Hearing this, Sufyān [al-Thawrī] said, 'How fortunate he is that it is not a liability but a gain!'[23]

Said Yaḥyā b. Muʿādh [al-Rāzī], 'Sincerity separates the [good] act from the offences just as the milk is separated from excretion and blood.'[C24]

[A] *Awliyā'*.

[B] By tradition, Muslim men are generally discouraged from wearing silk.

[C] Allusion to Qur'anic verse XVI.66 which describes how pure milk comes forth from the bellies of cows. See also the beginning of Chapter Seven below.

It is said that there was a man who used to go about dressed like a woman, attending every gathering of women—whether weddings or funerals. He chanced upon a place where a group of women was gathered. A pearl was stolen. The [women] exclaimed, 'Bolt the door that we may search.' And they searched the women one by one, until his turn came and that of a woman with him. He invoked God with sincerity, saying, 'If I am saved from this disgrace, I shall never do anything like it again.' The pearl was found with that woman, and a call rang out, 'Release the free-woman, we have found the pearl.'

Said a Sufi, 'I stood with Abū ʿUbayd al-Tustarī[25] as he tilled his soil following the afternoon prayers, on the day of ʿArafa. One of his vicar brethren (*ikhwānihi al-abdāl*)[A] came by and whispered something to him. Abū ʿUbayd replied, "No," and like a cloud the man went away, brushing off the earth, until he disappeared from my eyesight. I asked Abū ʿUbayd what [the man] said to him.

[A] *Badal* essentially refers to the substitution of anything or anyone by another, whether in person (Sufism) or by way of the permutative (grammar). When Sufis refer to the substitution of one attribute for another, they give a special sense to the conditional exchange whereby a new attribute is received from on high and another shed. If the reference is to people, then only seven individuals in the world can be said to be *abdāl* (sing., *badal*) at any one time. ʿAbd al-Razzāq al-Qāshānī's definition of *badal* agrees with Ibn ʿArabī's on the point about the possibility of action without motion. Physically speaking, that would be strange or superstitious, if not for the insights of Arabic linguistics and grammar, where *badal* is identified syntactically among the noun modifiers, or *tawābiʿ*. *Badal* has the advantage of standing independently for the noun it modifies, which allows the operation to act like a 'substitute' in the first place based on two devices, *kull min kull* and *baʿḍ min kull*. Grammatically, *tabdīl* is considered an offshoot of *tabaʿiyya* (subordination), which includes the permutative and other noun modifiers (*tawābiʿ*) like *naʿt* (descriptive adjective) and *ʿaf al-bayān* (explicative), which inform about or define a thing. Inexplicably, modern academics have largely ignored these antecedents. Sufis and philosophers have, however, long shared their linguistic inspirations across disciplinary boundaries (see my own work, *Thinking in the Language of Reality*). Linguistics seems to bind different dimensions of thinking considered by the practitioners of Sufism and the philosophers to be of great import, shedding interesting light on the practical mechanics behind Ghazālī's own thoughts.

'"He asked me to go on the pilgrimage with him and I declined."

'"Why did you not go?" I asked.

'"I lacked an intention to go on pilgrimage. I intended to finish [tilling] this soil by tonight. I feared going on pilgrimage with him for his sake—it would have exposed me to God's aversion, since I may have introduced into an act [devoted to] God something other than God. What I am now attending to is more imposing for me than seventy pilgrimages."'[26]

A man reportedly told, 'I went on a [military] sea expedition and one of us displayed a fodder sack. I thought I should buy it and avail myself of it during my expedition; when I enter such-and-such a city, I shall sell it and profit from it. So I bought it. But that night I saw in my sleep two persons descended from Heaven, as it were. One of them said to his companion, "Record the expedition," and he dictated to the latter,[27] "So-and-so [came for] amusement; so-and-so for ostentation; so-and-so for commerce; so-and-so in the way of God." Then he looked at me and said, "Write so-and-so went for commerce."

'"O God, O God! I plead my case," said I. "I went not to make commerce—I have nothing to trade. I went on a military expedition."

'"Sire, yesterday you purchased a sack by which you were hoping to profit," he said, and I wept.

'"Do not record me as a trader!"

'The man turned to his companion. "What is your mind?"

'"Write so-and-so went as a fighter, but on his way purchased a sack for profit—until God Almighty rules on it as He pleases."'[28]

Said Sarī al-Saqaṭī, 'Praying two *rakʿa*s of ritual prayer in private, both with sincerity, is better for you than committing seventy traditions to writing'—or 'seven hundred', 'or more'.[29]

A man said, 'In an hour's sincerity is salvation for eternity. Yet sincerity is rare.'[30]

It is said that knowledge is the seed, action its sowing, and that watering is sincerity. It is also said that when God is displeased with a servant, He offers him three things and denies him three. He offers him the friendship of the righteous but denies him their acceptance of him. He offers him righteous acts but denies him sincerity in them. He offers him sagacity but denies him truthfulness in it.

Said [Abū Yaʿqūb] al-Sūsī, 'God wishes only sincerity from the action of men.'[31]

Junayd, 'God has servants who reason; when they reason they act. When they act they are sincere. Sincerity summons them to all the doors of godliness.'[32]

Said Muḥammad b. Saʿīd [b. Ibrāhīm] b. al-Marwazī, 'The whole matter may be traced to two principles: God acting upon you and you acting for Him. You being content with what He does and you being sincere in what you do. Therefore, you will be happy with both and successful in the two abodes.[A] It depends entirely on contentment and sincerity—and precisely this makes for oneness (*tawḥīd*).'[33]

[A] Of heaven and earth.

CHAPTER SEVEN

An Exposition of the Reality of Sincerity

KNOW THAT ANYTHING apt to mingle with something else may, if cleansed and purified of it, be called pure (*khāliṣ*). The act of cleaning which purifies is called purification [or sincerity, *ikhlāṣ*].[A] God has said, *Between excretion and blood, milk pure and pleasant [do We give] to those who drink.*[B1] Thus, that milk is pure means that it is untarnished by blood and excretion, or anything that can mix with it.

Purifying (*ikhlāṣ*)[C] is the opposite of associating (*ishrāk*). He who is not pure [or sincere] (*mukhliṣ*) associates. However, association (*shirk*) occurs in degrees.[D] Association with respect to divinity is the opposite of sincerity (*ikhlāṣ*) with respect to oneness (*tawḥīd*). Association may be hidden or manifest, just like sincerity—although sincerity and its opposite occur in the heart, the locus being the heart in respect of purpose and intention.

[A] This clearly establishes that sincerity is an act, not just a state; and further, that in its root sense it is an act of self-purification.

[B] That is, the sincerity of his sincerity. Sūsī also said, 'The act which is truly sincere is that which is known neither by an angel, to record it, nor by any devil, to corrupt it, nor by the soul, to take pride in it' (Kalābādhī, *The Doctrine of the Sufis* 91).

[C] Or 'making sincere' through self-purification. This play on words does not have the same effect in English.

[D] *Shirk* (association [with God]) directly contradicts the 'unity of God' (*tawḥīd*), the most fundamental principle and one that governs all thinking in Islam, including philosophy. Ghazālī portrays the lack of sincerity as a form of association with God, because it involves mixing. He returns to *shirk* and *tawḥīd* in Chapter Ten.

We have considered the reality of intention in reference to the response to motives. So long as there is a single motive only,[2] the act that springs from it[3] is said to be sincerity (*ikhlāṣ*) relative to what is intended.

Therefore, he who gives alms strictly for show is 'sincere' (*mukhliṣ*).[A] He who aims to draw near to God (Exalted is He) is 'sincere'. However, the term 'sincerity' by custom signifies the aim—from which all stains are disserved—of drawing near to God. By the same token, deviation (*ilḥād*) is an 'inclination', although by convention it is an inclination away from truth.

The man motivated strictly by ostentation is liable to perish. We need not discuss him, as we already have[4] in the *Book of Ostentation*, the section on ruinous things.[5] The least that can be said in his case is what has been reported—namely, that on the day of resurrection the ostentatious person will be called forth by four names: O ostentatious one, O impostor, O idolater, O denier. For now, we shall discuss the one who, while motivated by the goal of drawing near [to God], mixes another motive with this, whether that of ostentation or something else attributable to the soul.

An example of this is when one fasts in order to benefit from the regimen that accompanies the fast, while aiming to draw near [to God]; or, when one frees a slave to be done with the whole burden [of his care] or the slave's ill temper. Or, when one takes a pilgrimage to improve his disposition through the movement of travel; to be rid of the harm to which he has been subjected in his country; to escape[6] a foe inside his household; or because he is annoyed with family and children, or some work he is doing and from which he wishes to take pause for a few days. Perhaps he wants to leave for war, learning its methods[7] and mobilising and leading soldiers in pursuit of battle. At night, [he may want] to pray, with the goal of suppressing the drowsiness in him, in order to watch over his family or belongings. He may want to gain knowledge to facilitate his search for adequate wealth, to find

[A] That is, sincere to his intention.

distinction[8] among his kin, or to keep his property or wealth protected from greed by dint of [his] knowledge. He may occupy himself with teaching and preaching to escape the torment of silence and to relish conversation. He may pledge himself in the service of the learned or the Sufis to raise amply their and other people's esteem of him; or to receive kindness in this world.

He may copy [the Qur'ān] in order to ameliorate his hand through diligent writing. He may wish to make the pilgrimage on foot to spare himself a rented [mount]. He may perform ablutions to clean or cool himself off; wash to give himself an agreeable scent; relate a tradition identified in a complete transmission chain; live secluded in a mosque to avoid renting a dwelling; fast to spare himself frequent cooking of food, or to free himself for his preoccupations, un-distracted by food; give alms to the beggar to end his wearisome begging; visit an ailing person that he, in turn, be visited should he fall ill; attend a funeral that the funerals of his own family be attended. He may do any of these just to be known by his good works, remembered and regarded for his probity and dignity.

But however much he is motivated to draw near to God, one of the thoughts above may impinge upon him and his act may be made easier due to [any] of these reasons. His act would then overstep the limit of sincerity, as it is no longer sincere for God's countenance. The association of [things with God] penetrates him.[9] But God has said, 'No one needs partnership less than I.'[10]

Briefly, the self finds ease in every worldly fortune and the heart inclines towards it, in scarcity or plenty. If [the self] proceeds to [thus] act, its purity is clouded—with this, sincerity is effaced. Man is attached to his fortunes and sunken in his appetites. Seldom is an act or devotion disengaged from temporal fortunes or goals of this type. This is why it is said, 'He who offers up but a single sincere moment of his life for God alone[A] shall be saved.'[11] This is because of the rarity of sincerity and the difficulty

[A] *Lit.*, 'God's face'.

of cleansing the heart from such blemishes. No, the sincere person is someone whose only motive is seeking to draw near to God. If the motive is [worldly] fortunes alone, then this is indeed a serious matter for this person. However, our concern is when the original purpose is to draw near [to God], and to it are added the above motives. These blemishes are of the rank of 'accompaniment', 'association' or 'assistance'—as mentioned earlier in the *Exposition on Intention.*[A12]

In sum, personal motive may be either similar to the religious motive, stronger or weaker—each judged differently from the other, as will be discussed later.

Sincerity is the purification of action of all the blemishes—whether few or many—until the goal becomes exclusively to draw near to God, with no other motive. This is possible only of someone enamoured and fond of God, and who is so engrossed in concentration on the Hereafter that the love of this world no longer sways his heart—to the point even that he has no liking for food or drink. On the contrary, his desire for it is akin to his wish to fill the need, insofar as it is an exigency of nature. Therefore, he does not desire food because it is food, but because it strengthens him in his worship of God. He hopes that[13] if he satisfies the evil of hunger, to the point of having no need of food, there will not remain in his heart anything exceeding what is necessary [for life]. He seeks only the measure of necessity, because this is what is necessary for his religion. Therefore, he has no other concern than God. Whether such a person eats or drinks, or satisfies his need, his action is sincere, his intention true in his every movement and rest. For example, when he sleeps for rest, with a view to strengthening his worship after that, his very sleep is [an act of] worship; for he is of the level of the sincere in this.

In the case of someone for whom [the above] does not hold true, the door of sincerity in action is barred, save on rare

[A] Ghazālī is referring to the divisions of the motives of the intention in Chapter Two above.

occasions. The habitual activities of someone dominated by the love of God and the Hereafter acquire the attribute of his preoccupation, becoming sincerity. The activities of someone whose soul is dominated by this world, by grandeur and by supremacy—in short, 'everything other than God'—acquire just this attribute.[A] Seldom are his devotions—fasting, prayer, etc.—ever accepted.

The remedy of sincerity (*ʿilāj al-ikhlāṣ*) consists in arresting the gratification of the self, ending the craving for this world, and being exclusively devoted to the Hereafter—thus letting the Hereafter dominate the heart, as this makes sincerity possible.

How many an act has man troubled himself with, thinking it sincere with respect to God. Yet, it contains vanity the harm of which he cannot see. It is told that one man recounted, 'I have for thirty years performed prayers at the mosque in the front row. One day, after being delayed for some reason, I prayed in the second row. I was gripped by shame before people because[14] they saw me in the second row. I then understood that I had unwittingly found in my heart joy and a reason for comfort with people looking at me at the first row.'

This is subtle and difficult to discern. Seldom are similar acts accepted. And rare[15] is the person alert to this, save the one to whom God has given success. Those who are unaware of it will in the Hereafter find all their good deeds bad. These are the people intended by God's words, *And before them shall appear plain what they had not reckoned; and before them shall appear the evil they have wrought*;[16] *Say: Shall we tell thee of those lost for their actions; those whose efforts are lost in the life of this world and who think they do good by their works.*[17]

Those who are subjected most severely to this trial are the scholars (*ʿulamāʾ*). Most are motivated to profess knowledge for the [mere] pleasure of [their] mastery, the joy of [gaining] a following and of being lauded and eulogised. The devil overlays them with this, for he says, 'Your goal is to proclaim God's religion, defend the revealed law which God's Messenger enacted.'

[A] Namely, the attribute of 'worshipping what is other than God.'

Consider the preacher who offers advice to people about God and counsels rulers. He is overjoyed at people's acceptance of him and his utterances. He claims to rejoice in having been chosen to serve religion. But should one of his peers who preaches better than he appear and people turn away from him, accepting the other, it would displease and distress him. Had religion been his motive, he would have thanked God, for God has spared him this weighty [obligation] through another.

In this, the devil will not let him be. He will say, 'Your distress is because reward was withheld from you, not because people turned their sights away from you and towards another—for had your words been preached to them, you would be the one rewarded. Your distress for being passed over for the reward is commendable.' The beggar is unaware that being bound by truth and relinquishing the matter is better;[18] it brings more ample reward and is more availing in the Hereafter than standing out [in this world].

Would that I knew whether ᶜUmar (may God be pleased with him) was distressed that Abū Bakr (may God be pleased with him) rather than he was to assume the leadership[19], and if is was praiseworthy or blameworthy! No man of religion could doubt that, had it been so,[A] it would have been blameworthy, because[20] being bound to the truth and relinquishing the matter to someone more appropriate than he is more availing in religion than an air of concern for people's welfare, however large the reward.

On the contrary, ᶜUmar rejoiced over the precedence of he who was more worthy than him of the matter. What then of the scholars who do not rejoice over similar things? A learned person is misled by the devil's deceptions. He tells himself that should anyone superior to him emerge, he would be happy for him. However, believing this of himself without trial and experience is sheer ignorance and delusion. The soul easily makes promises of this sort before anything has even transpired; and then, when

[A] That is, had ᶜUmar been distressed by the preferment of Abū Bakr.

it finally befalls him he changes and retracts, leaving the promise unfulfilled.

Only someone well-acquainted with the ruses of the devil and the soul—one who has long occupied himself with examining it [the soul]—knows this. Knowledge of the reality of sincerity and acting by it is, therefore, a deep ocean in which most people drown—save the odd or lone individual. The latter is the one whom God excepted, *Except Thy servants among them who are sincere*.[21]

Let then the servant of God be strict in his introspection and vigilance with respect to these subtle matters—barring which one will unwittingly succumb to following the devil.

CHAPTER EIGHT

An Exposition of What the Great Masters have Said About Sincerity

SAID [ABŪ YAʿQŪB] AL-SŪSĪ, 'Sincerity precludes seeing sincerity. The person who sees sincerity in his sincerity needs to purify his sincerity.'[A1]

What he said points to the purification of action from the vanity in action. Vanity is to take notice and to look at [one's own] sincerity. It is a flaw. The sincere person may be free of all flaws but he may be exposed to [this] one flaw.

Sahl al-Tustarī has said, 'Sincerity is when the servant's rest and movement are specifically for the sake of God.'[2] This is meant as a general statement. It implies what Ibrāhīm b. Adham said, 'Sincerity is truthfulness of intention with God.'[3]

Sahl al-Tustarī was once asked what was the most difficult [thing] for the soul. He answered, 'Sincerity, because the soul has no share in it.'[B4]

Said Ruwaym [b. Aḥmad al-Baghdādī], 'Sincerity in practice means that the one possessing it wants no recompense in either abode.'[C5]

[A] That is, the sincerity of his sincerity. Sūsī also said, 'The act which is truly sincere is that which is known neither by an angel, to record it, nor by any devil, to corrupt it, nor by the soul, to take pride in it' (Kalābādhī, *The Doctrine of the Sufis* 91).

[B] We have translated *naṣīb* here as 'share' but below as 'self-interest', since Ghazālī takes the self's claims to any share as something that mixes with and therefore tarnishes the sincerity of acting solely for God.

[C] That is, in either this world or the next.

This signifies that the soul's share is a flaw in this world and the next. The worship of the person who seeks gratification of the soul's appetite in Paradise is marred. The truth is that—in one's actions—nothing but God's countenance ought to be wished for. This is a definition of the sincerity of the perfectly sincere (*ṣiddīqīn*)—and this is absolute sincerity.

As to he who acts in expectation of Paradise and in fear of Hellfire, he is sincere in comparison to he who seeks his immediate needs [in this life]; otherwise, his search is for ease and a full stomach. But for people of insight the true object of search is God's countenance alone.[6]

There is the objection[7] that man is motivated solely for his share; that freedom from any share is an attribute of divinity and whoever lays claim to it is a non-believer.

The Qādī Abū Bakr al-Baqillānī ruled that whoever claims to be free of [the desire for his] share is a non-believer. He maintained that this is one of the attributes of divinity. What Baqillānī said is true, but what the Sufis mean by it is the freedom from[8] what people call 'shares'—namely, desirable [things] stipulated solely for Paradise. As to the pleasure of knowledge, intimate discourse (*munājāt*) and the sight of God's countenance, these are their proper share. Yet, people do not regard this as a share; rather, they marvel [that] it [should be so]. If they [the Sufis] were to given all the comforts of Paradise in exchange for that pleasure they derive from obedience, intimate discourse and the experience (*shuhūd*) which attends divine presence (*lil-ḥaḍra al-ilāhīya*), openly and secretly, they would disdain and ignore them. Therefore, they are moved[A] for the sake of a share and they obey for the sake of a share, though their share is He whom they worship and no other.

Said Abū ʿUthmān [al-Nīsābūrī], 'Sincerity is to be oblivious to the sight of creation alone through the abiding gaze at the Creator.'[9] This points only to the flaw of ostentation. This is

[A] *Ḥaraka* literally means movement. However, in theology, philosophy and common Arabic usage it implies motive, the factor that precipitates the action.

why one man said, 'Sincerity of action is what the devil has not descried and so cannot vitiate, and what no angel [has descried] and so will not be record—for it signifies strict concealment.'[A]

It is said that sincerity is what is hidden from created beings and purified of attachments. This better encompasses the meanings intended.

Said [al-Ḥārith b. Asad] al-Muḥāsibī, 'Sincerity is the withdrawal of the created being from the [necessity of] reciprocation from the Lord.' And this signifies the absence of ostentation.

Likewise, [Ibrāhīm b. Aḥmad] al-Khawwāṣ said, 'He who drinks from the cup of servanthood (*ka'is al-ʿibāda*) leaves the sincerity of worship.'

The Apostles asked Jesus, 'Who is pure (*khāliṣ*) in action?' He said, 'He who acts[10] for the sake of God without longing for anyone's praise.'[11] This, too, has to do with abandoning ostentation. But it was singled out because it is the strongest cause of the blurring of sincerity.

Said Junayd, 'Sincerity is the act cleansed of all turbidity.'[12]

Said al-Fuḍayl, 'Forgoing an act for the sake of people is ostentation, whereas acting for the sake of people is idolatry. Sincerity is when God spares you from both.'[13]

It is said that sincerity is perpetual vigilance and the disregard of fortunes.[14]

This is evidence in full. There are many utterances on this matter. However, voluminous copying is of no further use once the truth has been revealed. The proof that suffices is that of the master of the ancients and contemporaries alike, may God bless him and grant him peace.[B] For when he was asked about sincerity, he said, 'It is to say: My Lord is God; then to be upright as you were enjoined'[15]—that is, that you do not worship your desires

[A] According to Junayd, sincerity is a secret between God and the servant that no angel knows [for the purpose] of recording it, no devil vitiates it...' (*Qūt* II:152; Qushayrī, *Risāla*, '*Ikhlāṣ*' 163; cf. Zabīdī 55).

[B] The Prophet Muḥammad.

and your self, that you worship none but your Lord, and you be upright in worship as you have been enjoined. This indicates the exclusion of what is other than God from one's purview. This is true sincerity.

CHAPTER NINE

An Exposition of the Levels of Blemishes and Flaws that Cloud Sincerity

KNOW THAT SOME flaws which confound sincerity are plain; some are concealed, some weak despite their plainness and others strong despite their concealment. The difference in levels of plainness and latency may be understood only through an example.

First level: The most conspicuous flaw confounding sincerity is ostentation. By way of example, let us say: the devil can cause someone's prayer to be flawed, no matter how sincere that person's may be. If a group of people are watching him or someone approaches him, he [the devil] will say to him, 'Make good your prayer so that those in attendance may look upon you with reverence and piety and that they may neither scorn nor slander you.' Thus, he is humbled in his limbs, his extremities are stilled and his prayer becomes comely. This is plain ostentation, and it is not lost on the beginners among the disciples.[A]

Second level: Understanding this flaw and being wary of it, the disciple neither hearkens to the devil nor gives him notice, and he continues to pray as before. He [the devil] then approaches him with a show of goodness. He speaks, 'You are followed and imitated. You are highly regarded. Whatever you do is told about you. Others emulate you, so if their works are good you will be rewarded for them. But the burden is on you, should you do wrong. Therefore, perform good works in their presence. It may

[A] *Murīdūn* (sing. *murīd*), derives from the same radical as 'intention' (*irāda*).

be that they will imitate you in humility and improvement of worship.'

This level is less clear than the first. He who is not misled by the first is apt to be misled here; for this too is nothing but ostentation and it invalidates sincerity. If the person regards humility and correct worship as good, he would not want others to relinquish. Why then does he not privately content himself with this? It cannot be that the soul of another person is more precious to him than his own. This is pure deception. The person followed is he who is upright in himself and whose heart is illuminated. Therefore, his light spreads onto others and he is rewarded for it. As for the former, his is pure hypocrisy and deception. Whoever follows his example will be rewarded for it. But as for him, he will be answerable for his deception and he will be punished for exhibiting a quality which is not his.

Third level: This level is more subtle than those above, in that the servant of God tests himself with it and descries the devil's stratagem. He knows that[1] any discrepancy between his privacy and visibility before others is mere ostentation. He knows that sincerity is when his private prayer resembles his public prayer. He would be ashamed of himself and shamed before his Lord should he be deferent to the gaze of his fellows more than what he is wont to do. In private, he turns his attention to himself, improving his prayer in a manner that would satisfy him in public and prays publicly in the same way. This, too, is hidden ostentation, since he has improved his private prayer in order to make his prayer comely in public, without distinguishing between them.[2] Whether in private or in public, he heeds only people.

Sincerity is when the gazes of the beasts or of people upon his praying are all of the same order. However, this person disallows the fouling of prayer in front of people; and yet, he is ashamed to appear in the image of the ostentatious, thinking that it is no longer germane because his prayer is the same in private as in public.[3] Far from it! It ceases to be germane only when he ignores people and inanimate objects, both in private and public.[4] Yet, this person is preoccupied with people both in private and public. This is among the devil's secret ruses.

Fourth level: This is the subtlest and most hidden level. It occurs when people look at the person in prayer but the devil is powerless to tell him, 'Be deferent in front of them.' This is because the devil knows that he understands this,[5] and so the devil tells him, 'Think of the greatness of God Exalted and Majestic. Who are you to stand before Him? How shameful for you that He should see your heart while it is heedless of Him.' The man takes this to heart, his every limb in deference, believing this to be the essence of sincerity, while all along it is the very essence of artifice and deceit.

Had his deference come from seeing God's majesty, this notion would have accompanied him in private; it would not be present solely whenever others are present.[6] A sign of being secure from this flaw is that the notion he conjures up in private resemble what he conjures up in a crowd, and that the presence of other people did not give rise to the notion, any more than the presence of the beast might be its cause. As long as the person distinguishes, in what concerns him, between the sight of a man and the sight of a beast, he departs from pure sincerity. He defiles the interior with idolatry hidden by ostentation. This idolatry is more concealed in man's heart than 'the black ant crawling in a dark night across a hard rock,' as the report goes.[7]

He is saved from the devil whose view is refined and who is fortuned with God's protection and the success and guidance He bestows. For, the devil clings to those in assiduous[8] worship of God. He will not leave them one moment without inciting them to ostentation at every turn—such as the darkening of the eyelids with *kohl*, trimming of whiskers, perfuming on Friday or donning of [good] clothes. Those Prophetic practices (*sunan*) are sanctioned for particular occasions; from them a hidden benefit accrues to the soul, because people are bound to look at the person and because they are congenial to [human] nature.[9] Therefore, the devil will urge the person to practice them, saying, 'This is *Sunna*.

You ought not abandon it.' Interiorly, the heart is incited to [their practice] because of such a hidden desire; or because of a blemish which has tarnished it beyond the limit of sincerity.

Whoever is not free of[10] all of these flaws is not pure of sincerity (*khāliṣ*). On the contrary, the devil [for example] causes the person retreating to a filled mosque that is clean, beautifully built and congenial to [his] nature, impressing upon him all the more the virtues of retreat. The *mover* (*muḥarrik*) concealed inside him is both the congeniality of the mosque's beautiful form[11] and the setting of his heart upon it. This is plain from the person's inclination towards one of two mosques or locations[12] if it is more beautiful than the other. But all that is tarnish from the blemishes of [human] nature, turbidity of the soul and vitiation of the essence of sincerity.

By the life of me, the cheating that blends [extraneous substances] with pure gold [coins] is of different levels. [At one level,] the dominant [substance] prevails; at another, the lesser but still easily perceptible; at yet another, what is so subtle that none but a keen numismatist can perceive it. The cheating of the heart, the corruption of the devil and the wickedness of the soul are far subtler and more dubious. This is why it is said, 'Two *rakʿas* by a learned person are better than a year's worship by an ignorant one.'[13] By this, I mean the learned person who sees the subtle flaws of actions and purifies himself of them. The ignorant man sees only the appearance of worship and its deception, just as the boor sees the redness and roundness of the impure *dinar* coin which is fake and counterfeit in itself. A carat of pure [gold] that the keen numismatist[14] approves is better than the *dinar* approved by someone gullible and dim-witted.

This is how those who perform[15] acts of worship are differentiated; nay, even more so. The ways in which flaws impinge on the varieties of conduct are limitless—countless. May what we have said by way of example give benefit. For the few [words] rather than the many suffice the astute, whereas no amount shall satisfy the stupid. Therefore, further elaboration would serve no use.

CHAPTER TEN

An Exposition on the Judgement of the Tarnished Act and the Worthiness of the Reward for it

KNOW THAT WHEN action is not [made] sincere for the sake of God but, on the contrary, is mixed with the taint of ostentation or self-interest, people disagree[1] on whether it deserves a reward, a punishment or nothing at all and thus is neither to one's benefit nor to one's detriment.

As to that whose intention was nothing but ostentation, it definitely incurs a liability and it is the reason for the odium and punishment [of God]. While what is sincere for the sake of God is the reason for the reward. With respect to the tarnished [act], the reports explicitly point out that there is no reward for it. However, the reports are not without contradiction in this.

Useful to us in this [matter]—though [all] knowledge [ultimately] is with God (Exalted is He)—is the consideration of the amount of motivational power.[2] Thus, if the religious motive is equal to the personal motive—each balancing the other out, the act will neither be to his benefit nor to his detriment. If the motive for ostentation preponderates and is more powerful—the [religious motive] will not avail. In this respect, it [the motive for ostentation] is harmful and leads[3] to punishment. Nevertheless, the penalty for it is lighter than for an act intended strictly as ostentation and in which there is no hint of drawing near [to God].

If the intention to draw near to God prevails, compared to another motive, there is a reward to the measure of the prevalence of the religious motive. For God has said, *Then anyone who has done an atom's weight of good shall see it. And anyone who has done an atom's weight of evil shall see it*[4]; and, *God wrongs not an atom's weight. But if it be goodness, He doubles it.*[5]

Therefore, the good intention will not be lost. When it prevails over the intention of ostentation, the amount [of ostentation] equivalent to it will be foiled and the surplus [good intention] will remain. But when it is subordinated, it nonetheless cancels something from the vain intention's punishment. This is laid bare by the fact that actions influence the hearts by confirming their attributes. The motive for ostentation is deleterious, and what nourishes and strengthens something deleterious is action that agrees with it. [On the other hand,] the motive for the good is delivered and strengthened by action appropriate to it. Therefore, if the two attributes are in the heart together, they conflict. When an act complies with the requirement of ostentation, this attribute is strengthened. When the act complies with the requirement of the approach to God, this attribute is in turn strengthened. While one [attribute] is deleterious, the other is salutary.

When the strengthening of the one is proportional to the strengthening of the other, counterbalancing each other, it is much like someone suffering from a fever, having contracted something harmful.[6] Then he receives a cooling palliative to counterbalance the power of the latter; then, upon receiving it, he will be as if he had not received anything.[A] However, if one is more dominant, it is not without effect.

Just as not an atom's weight of food, drink and medicament is lost, and is not without effect on the body by way of God's *sunna*, so not an atom's weight of either good or evil is lost. It is not without effect in the illumination of the heart or its darkening, and the drawing near to or separation from God. Therefore, if a person draws near[7] by just a span of the hand, and withdraws by a span of the hand,[8] he will have returned to where he was—with

[A] That is, not received either what was harmful or what has cured him. Together they return him to his original state.

no benefit or detriment. If the act brings him nearer by two spans and distances him a single span, he will be left with one span.

Said the Prophet (may God bless him and grant him peace), 'Let a good deed follow the sin, effacing it.'[9] Thus[10] pure ostentation[11] will be effaced when followed by pure sincerity. But if they are joined together they perforce repel each other.

The consensus of the community attests to this in that the pilgrimage of the person who sets out as a pilgrim but engages in commerce is sound and will be requited, even if it be mixed with certain self-interest. Admittedly, one may object that the pilgrim is requited but only for acts performed for the pilgrimage upon reaching Mecca. Since [the pilgrim's] commerce does not depend on this, he is sincere, even if what he associates [with the pilgrimage] lasts the entire duration[A] and will not requited so long as the intended purpose is to do commerce. Nevertheless, the correct view is that so long as the pilgrimage is the primary moving [cause] and the commerce is intended as an aid or supplement,[12] then the distance travelled itself will not be without reward.

In my opinion, fighters make no discernible mental distinction between fighting the unbelievers with a view to the spoils that might accrue to them and fighting in a manner that brings no booty. One cannot well say that discerning this generally defeats the reward for doing battle. It is more proper to say that when the primary motive and strong rousing [factor] is the elevation of God's word, and when the desire for booty is secondary, the reward will not be lost. Indeed, the reward of that fighter is not the same as the reward of one whose heart is turned toward the booty, as this no doubt is a deficiency.

One may argue that the verses of the Qur'ān and the reports indicate that the flaw of ostentation defeats the reward, and that this includes the seeking of booty, commerce and other benefits. Ṭā'ūs [b. al-Kaysān al-Yamānī] and others[13] among the succeeding generation (*al-Tābiʿūn*) told about a man who asked the Prophet about another who performed good deeds—or he may have said

[A] Literally, 'lasts the entire distance'.

'who gives alms'—and longed to be praised and rewarded. The Prophet knew not what to make of what he was told, until it was revealed to him, *He who expects to meet his Lord, let him do a righteous act, and let him commit no idolatry in his worship of the Lord.*[14] He meant both reward and praise.[15]

Muᶜādh [b. Jabal] related that the Prophet had said, 'The smallest measure of ostentation is idolatry.'[16]

Said Abū Hurayra, 'The Prophet said, "The one who commits idolatry in his worship will be told: Take your requital from whomever you have acted for."'[17]

From ᶜIbāda [b. al-Ṣāmit] it is related[A] that God Almighty and Majestic said, 'No one needs partnership less than I. Whoever performs a deed for My sake[18] while associating another with Me, I cede my part to My partner.'[19]

Said Abū Mūsā [al-Ashᶜarī] recounted that a nomadic Arab[B] went to God's Messenger and told him, 'O Messenger of God, a man fights because of anger, a man fights because of courage, a man fights that he may be seen [as brave]. Which of them is in the path of God?' God's Messenger told him, 'Whoever fights for God's word to be supreme—he is in God's path.'[20]

On this [matter] ᶜUmar recounted, 'You say that this person was martyred. But maybe he filled both sides of his mount with [sackfuls of] silver pieces.'[21]

Ibn Masᶜūd said about it,[22] 'The Messenger of God said that by migrating with the aspiration for something of this world, one migrates for that alone.'[23]

We maintain that these traditions do not contradict what we have said, their purpose being [to refer to] he who therewith desires only the world—as in the [Messenger's] words 'migrating with the aspiration for something of this world'—that was the

[A] That is, in the words of the Prophet.

[B] *Aᶜrābiyyan*, which means a nomad who speaks in the Arabic tongue—a desert 'Arab' or Bedouin, as we might commonly say today. 'Arab' as an ethnic designation has no basis in classical Arabic.

person's dominant concern. We mentioned that this is disobedience and enmity, not because worldly pursuit is forbidden but because worldly pursuit in religious activity is forbidden, contains ostentation and amounts to misplaced worship.

Wherever the term partnership (*shirka*)[A] is found, it has to do with equality. We have demonstrated that two equal intentions balance each other out. There is neither benefit nor detriment; therefore, one ought to expect no reward.

Thus, with partnership man[24] is ever in peril, for he knows not which of two things dominates over his intention. This is deleterious for him. It is why God Almighty has said, *He who expects to meet his Lord, let him do a righteous act, and let him commit no idolatry*[B] *in his worship of the Lord.*[25] In other words, meeting [Him] cannot be expected by way of partnership, the outcome of which is, at best, a falling away.

One may object that the rank of martyrdom is attainable only through sincerity in warfare. But this is not to say that a person whose religious motive stirs him to engage in war [for Islam] even if there were no booty,[26] and he is capable of fighting two groups of unbelievers—one wealthy, the other poor—and he leans toward the wealthy with a view to both elevating the word of God and [taking] the spoils, that such a person will surely not be rewarded for his fighting.[27] God forbid that it should be so! In religion, this would be narrow, leading the Muslims to despair, because no human being, save the rare ones, ever extricates himself of secondary flaws like these. This occasions a diminution of the reward and consequently its thwarting. Nay!

Granted, man is in great peril in this, because he may believe that the purpose of drawing near to God is his strongest motive, although his dominant motive in secret is self-interest. This counts among the most deeply hidden [motives].

[A] For the implications of this term, see footnote on *shirk* (association/partnership) and *tawḥīd* in Chapter Seven above.

[B] *Yushrik*, i.e., 'associating God with any partner'.

Therefore, there can be no recompense (*ajar*) save through sincerity. And the servant of God is rarely certain of his own sincerity, however cautious he may be. This is why, on completion of his effort, he should always waver between rejection and acceptance,[A] fearful of a flaw in his worship the evil outcome of which might be greater than any reward. Hence, the fearful are discerning, and this is how every discerning person should be.

Thus, Sufyān [al-Thawrī] said, 'I ignore what comes of my action.'[B]

And said ʿAbd al-ʿAzīz b. Abī Dā'ūd,[28] 'For sixty years I have lived close to this House[C]; and sixty times have I gone on pilgrimage. Never have I undertaken any activity [for the sake of] God without examining myself. I found the devil's part more ample than God's. If only it were neither benefit nor detriment for me.'[29]

Nevertheless, one must not avoid action for fear of fault and ostentation,[30] for that is the greatest wish of the devil. The aim is not to forsake sincerity. Whenever action is abandoned, both the action and the sincerity are together lost.

It is told that a devotee was in the service of Abū Saʿīd al-Kharrāz, hard at work. One day Abū Saʿīd spoke of sincerity,[31] meaning sincerity in work. So the devotee took to examining his heart with every activity and demanding of it sincerity. But, to his master's loss, he found it difficult to fill his obligations. Abū Saʿīd then asked him what was the matter. [The man] informed him about the reality of sincerity he demanded of himself, that

[A] In other words, never make a categorical decision that God will either reject or accept his act.

[B] '*Lā aʿtadd*'—in '*lā aʿtadd bi-mā ẓahara min ʿamalī*'—refers obliquely to the Hereafter, as Makkī makes clear in the *Qūt* 163; the 'reward' there remains hidden. In the context of the *Qūt*, which Zabīdī (p. 64) identifies as the source of this saying by Sufyān, Makkī compares sincerity to the action that flows from it and to the purpose of the action in God, according to the dynamics between the *bāṭin* (hidden) and the *ẓāhir* [manifest]—hence, '*bi-mā* ẓahara' in the quotation.

[C] The House of God or the Kaʿba.

he was not equal to it in most of his activities, and that he thus relinquished them. Abū Saʿīd replied, 'Act not thus, for sincerity does not preclude the doing.[32] Therefore, persevere in action, endeavour to attain sincerity. I have not told thee to put activity aside, but to be sincere in your action!'[33]

Said al-Fuḍayl [b. ʿIyād], 'Forsaking action on account of people is ostentation. Action for the sake of people is idolatry (*shirk*).'[34]

PART III

ON TRUTHFULNESS, ITS MERIT AND REALITY

CHAPTER ELEVEN

An Exposition of the Merit of Truthfulness

GOD SAID, *There are men who have been true to their covenant with God.*[1] And the Prophet (may God bless him and grant him peace) said, 'Truthfulness (*ṣidq*) guides towards piety (*birr*) and piety guides towards Paradise. Verily, a man will be true until it shall be written with God that he is perfectly truthful (*ṣiddīq*). But mendacity leads to immorality and immorality to the Fire.[2] A man will lie until it shall be written with God that he is mendacious.'[3]

About the merit of truthfulness, suffice it to say that 'perfectly truthful person' (*ṣiddīq*) derives from it. God (Exalted is He) described thus the prophets by way of praise and extolment, *And recall from the Book that Ibrāhīm was a prophet perfectly truthful;*[4] *And recall from the Book that Ishmael was true to his promise* (*ṣādiq al-waʿd*), *a messenger and a prophet;*[5] *And recall from the Book that Idrīs was a prophet perfectly truthful.*[A6]

Said Ibn ʿAbbās, 'The four [traits] inside a person that profit him: truthfulness (*ṣidq*), modesty (*ḥayā'*), beauty of character (*ḥusn al-khuluq*) and gratitude (*shukr*).'[7]

Said Bishr b. al-Ḥārith [al-Ḥāfī], 'He who deals truthfully with God will be estranged from people.'[8]

Said Abū ʿAbd Allāh al-Ramlī, 'I saw Manṣūr al-Dīnawarī in a

[A] We have used the Arabic forms for the names of the ancient prophets mentioned in the above Qur'ānic verses: Ibrāhīm for Abraham, Ismāʿīl for Ishmael and Idrīs for Enoch.

dream. I asked him, "What has God done for you?" "He has forgiven me, had mercy upon me and given me what I had not hoped for," [Dīnawarī answered]. So I asked him, "And the best thing by which the servant turns to God—what is it?" "Truthfulness. And the worst thing by which he turns is mendacity," [he said].'[9]

Said Abū Sulaymān [al-Dārānī], 'Make truthfulness your mount, truth your sword[10] and God Almighty the goal of your desideration.'[11]

A man asked al-Ḥakīm, 'What is your view of truthfulness?' He replied, 'If you were truthful[12] you would recognise the truthful.'[13]

Muḥammad b. ʿAlī [b. Jaʿfar] al-Kattānī, 'We have found the religion of God to be built upon three pillars: truth, truthfulness and justice. The truth is borne by the limbs, justice by hearts and truthfulness by minds.'[14]

Regarding God's words, *On the day of judgement, you will see those who lied about God with blackened faces,*[15] al-Thawrī[16] said, 'They are those who claimed to love God but who were insincere in this.'[17]

God inspired [the Prophet] David, 'O David, whoever is true to Me in his innermost being, I shall be true to him before [all] men.'[18]

At a session of [Abū Bakr] Shiblī's, a man cried out and threw himself into the Tigris. Shiblī said, 'If he is truthful, God (Exalted is He) will save him, just as He saved Moses (may God grant him peace). If he lies, God (Exalted is He) will drown him as He did Pharaoh.'[19]

Another recounted, 'Jurists and scholars agree consensually on three traits. If sound, they bring deliverance and none is complete without the others: Islam free of deviation and desire; truthfulness with God (Exalted is He) in works, and properly gained nourishment.'[20]

Said Wahb b. Munabbih [al-Yamānī], 'I found on the margin of the Torah twenty-two items.[A] The righteous Children of Israel

[A] *Lit.*, 'letters' (*ḥurūf*).

gather to read and to study them. They are: no treasure more availing than knowledge; no possession more profitable than discernment; no noble birth more refined than good manners; no lineage more vulgar than rage; a mate more becoming than reason; no companion more disgraceful than ignorance; no rank dearer than godliness; no nobility more fulfilling[21] than forsaking desire; no action more virtuous than thinking; no deed better than patience; no evil more vile than pride; no remedy milder than kindness; no ailment more painful than foolishness; no messenger more just than the truth; no sign more trustworthy than truthfulness; no poverty more demeaning than greed; no wealth more unhappy than accumulation; no life more pleasant than health; no livelihood more felicitous than continence; no [act of] worship more comely than humility; no abstinence better than temperance; no safeguard more protecting than silence; and nothing closer than death.'[22]

Said Muḥammad b. Saᶜīd al-Marwazī, 'If you seek God truthfully, God Almighty shall give you[23] a mirror with which to see every marvel in this world and the next.'[24]

Said Abū Bakr al-Warrāq, 'Maintain truthfulness in everything between you and God (Exalted is He), and kindness in your dealings with people.'[25]

Dhū al-Nūn was asked, 'Is there a means for the servant of God to rectify his affairs?' He replied:

From sins we remain perplexed[26]
 Truthfulness we seek what way there is
And so the claims of desire upon us lighten
 as what is other than desire upon us weighs.[27]

Sahl [al-Tustarī] was asked, 'What is the origin of this matter before us?' He said, 'Truthfulness, generosity and courage.' 'Add to that,' he was told. 'Fear of God, modesty and properly [gained] nourishment.'[28]

From Ibn ᶜAbbās it is related that the Prophet was asked about perfection and said, 'Truth in speech and truthfulness in action.'[29]

About God's words, *That [God] may question the truthful about their truthfulness*,[30] Junayd held that God will ask those who are truthful to themselves about their truthfulness to their Lord, and that therein lies danger.[31]

CHAPTER TWELVE

An Exposition of the Reality of Truthfulness, Its Meaning and Levels

KNOW THAT THE term truthfulness (*ṣidq*) is used in six senses: truthfulness in speech (*qawl*); truthfulness in intention (*niyya*) and will (*irāda*); truthfulness in resolve (*ʿazm*); truthfulness in the fulfilment of resolve (*wafāʾ bi'l-ʿazm*); truthfulness in action (*ʿamal*); and truthfulness in the realisation of every religious station (*taḥqiq maqāmāt al-dīn*). Thus, someone who is ascribed all of these is 'perfectly truthful' (*ṣiddīq*), this being the most intense [form of] truthfulness. But these [senses], too, have levels. Whoever[1] has but a portion of truthfulness in any of the things [mentioned above] is truthful (*ṣādiq*) in relation to that in which he is truthful.

The first sense, truthfulness of the tongue, can only take place through uttering, or through that which the utterance contains and to which it alerts. The utterance may be linked to the past or the future, and pertain either to the fulfilment or breaking of a promise. It is incumbent upon every servant of God to keep to his word, speaking only truthfully. This is the best-known and most obvious type of truthfulness. Whoever holds his tongue from reporting things other than what they are—that person is truthful (*ṣādiq*).

However,[2] this [kind of] truthfulness has two perfections: The first[3] is to guard against equivocations. For it is said, 'Equivocation can be an alternative to lying;'[4] since it can take the place of lying. The peril of lying consists in explaining something in a way contrary to what that thing is in itself—unless required by the circumstances[5] and determined to be beneficial in a [particular] case; for the training of boys, women and like persons; as a precaution against[6] some wrong; or in the struggle against enemies to prevent them from espying the secrets of the realm. The truthfulness of a person constrained by any of these things is that his utterance in the latter be [for the sake of] God, in whatever the truth commands or religion requires him to do. If he utters it, he is truthful, even if his words expound something other than that which is the case. This is because truthfulness [in speech] is desired, not for itself but, rather for an indication of the truth and its invocation; one does not consider its form but its meaning.

To be sure, in such a situation he ought to resort to equivocations so long as he must. When the Messenger of God set off on a trip he used to disguise himself as someone else, in order not to alert enemies who might pursue him.[7] But this is not being untruthful in anything. Said the Messenger, 'He is not a liar who reconciles between two [people]; it is said to be good or to increase the good.'[8] He [the Prophet] authorised this kind of speech in three cases whenever benefit is served: when one is reconciling between two [people], has two wives or has military considerations. Here, truthfulness is transferred to the intention, and nothing more is considered than the truthfulness of the intention and the desire for good. Whenever the purpose is sound, the intention truthful and the desire purely for the good, one is both truthful (*ṣādiq*) and perfectly truthful (*ṣiddīq*), regardless of what the utterance happens to be.

Thence, equivocation here is preferable. This approach is illustrated by the man who, being pursued by a miscreant at home, says to his wife, 'Draw a circle with your finger, place the finger upon the circle and say, "He is not here."'[A] In so doing, lying was avoided and the miscreant was warded off. Consequently, his words are truthful and the miscreant has understood that he is not at home.[9]

[A] The husband is referring to himself.

Thus, the first perfection [of truthfulness] in respect of speech is to avoid both candid utterance and equivocation except upon necessity.

The second perfection is to adhere to what truthfulness means in his utterances when he confides in the Lord, as in the words, *I have turned my face as a true [believer] towards He who created the heavens and the earth.*[10] Thus if his heart is turned away from God and is occupied with the longings and desires of this world, he is a liar.[11] Or the words, *Thee do we worship and from Thee do we seek help*;[12] or *I am the servant of God.*[13] Someone who is not ascribed the essence of servantship and has something other than God as his goal, his words are not truthful. And when on the Day of Judgement he is asked for truthfulness in his words 'I am the servant of God,' he will be unable to make good. If he has been a slave to himself, the world or his desires, he could not be true to his words.

A person is the servant of everything to which he is bound.[14] As Jesus (may God grant him peace) said, 'O worshippers of this world';[15] and as our Prophet (may God bless him and grant him peace) said, 'Wretched is the slave of wealth and the slave of money,[A] wretched is the slave of dress and the slave of the mantle.'[B16]

One is said to be the slave of that by which his heart is bound.[17] The true slave of God is he who is firstly manumitted from what is not God and made completely free. Then, when this freedom takes its course, the heart is emptied and servantship for God settles in it, occupying it with God and the love for God. The person's interior and exterior become bound by obedience to Him, and he has no other goal but God (Exalted is He). Then, one passes over to another, more sublime station called freedom. This is a manumission also from one's own will for [proximity to] God in so far as it is one's will.[18] The person contents himself with

[A] '*ʿAbd al-dīnār*' and '*ʿabd al-darham*'. 'Slave' and 'servant' are used interchangeably here to indicate both service and slavishness.

[B] That is, the mantle of recognition and authority bestowed upon a learned person or someone in an official position.

whatever God wills for him in proximity or from afar. His will vanishes in the will of God (Exalted is He).[19]

This is a slave manumitted from what is other than God, one who becomes free. He has relinquished and manumitted himself—he becomes free, absent to himself but present for his Master and Patron. If the [Master] moves him, he moves; if He keeps him at rest, he will stay at rest. If He puts him through trial, he will be content. There is no more room for desire, petition or contrariety.[20] Rather, he is before God as the dead are before the ritual washer [of the deceased].[21]

This is utmost truthfulness in servantship to God. The true servant is one who exists for his Patron, not for himself. This is the degree of those who are perfectly truthful (*ṣiddīqūn*). As to the degrees of the truthful (*ṣādiqūn*), it is freedom from what is other than God. Beyond these, servantship for God is realised. While whatever precedes this, does not merit the title of either truthful or perfectly truthful. This then is what truthfulness in speech means.

The second type of truthfulness, in respect of intention and will, is connected with sincerity—namely, that the only motive for movement or rest is God (Exalted is He). If a blemish of self-interest is mixed in with it, the truthfulness of intention will be vitiated. Whoever possesses it may be called a liar.[22] It is as we recounted with respect to the excellence of sincerity in the tradition about the three [men],[23] where the learned one was asked what he had done with what he learned, and he answered, 'I did such-and-such.' God then said, 'You lie—nay, you wished it be said only that this man is learned.' God did not disaffirm his [act] or say that the man did not act; he disaffirmed his will and intention.

Someone once said that truthfulness is sound [adherence to God's] Oneness (*tawḥīd*) in the intention.[24]

Similarly, God said, *God bears witness that the hypocrites are liars;*[25] when they said, 'Ye are the Messenger of God.' This is truthfulness.[A] However, their lie is not in respect of what they

[A] Meaning that they spoke the truth when affirming that the Prophet is the

uttered through the tongue, but in respect of what is innermost in their heart. Lying has to do with reporting. The utterance entails reporting about the connection with the state, since the speaker on his own wishes to show that he believes what he says.[26] That person lies in connection with his state based on what is in his heart. Therefore, he lies in *this*, not in what he uttered. Thus one sense of truthfulness refers to the purity of intention—namely, sincerity. Every truthful person then is perforce sincere.

The third type of truthfulness is the truthfulness of resolve.[27] Man puts resolve ahead of deed. He says to himself, 'If God provides me with money, I shall give either all or half of it in alms. If I encounter an enemy in the way of God, I shall fight. I am not chary about being killed. If God grants me authority, I shall be just in its exercise and never defy Him through any inequity or be drawn towards created beings.'

This is the resolution which he makes on his own—a decisive, honest resolution. In his resolve, a person may have a certain inclination, indecision and weakness which run against the truthfulness of the resolution. Truthfulness in this respect consists of perfection and capacity—as when one says of another that he possesses a true appetite, and of an ailing person[28] that his appetite belies, having no strong and constant cause, or that it is weak. This [here] is the application and intended meaning of truthfulness.

The beneficial resolution of a truthful or perfectly truthful person is, in its entirety, strong to perfection.[29] It contains no inclination, weakness or indecision. Rather, the soul always confers determined, unwavering resolve upon good works.

As ʿUmar (may God be pleased with him) said, 'Were I to be put forward, I prefer that my neck be struck than to govern a people with Abū Bakr [still] in their midst.' He found within himself firm resolve and sincere love—in refusing to govern in the presence of Abū Bakr.[A][30] He reaffirmed this in what he said about slaying.

messenger of God.

[A] This occurred on the Day of Saqīfa, when ʿUmar b. al-Khaṭṭāb was being

The levels of resolve among the perfectly truthful differ. There may be a resolve which does not lead to the acceptance of dying. However, if a person is not fully of a mind to come forward, his resolve will not end even if he should be reminded of the tradition on slaying. The perfectly truthful and the believing include those who, having to choose between Abū Bakr or their own slaying, would find their own life dearer than that of Abū Bakr the Truthful (*al-Ṣiddīq*).[31]

The fourth type of truthfulness is the fulfilment of resolve. The soul can be amply resolute at any given moment, for there is no difficulty in giving promise or having resolve. The onus is light in this. But when truths are actualised and consolidated, and the passions astir, then the will is relaxed and the passions prevail—which does not accord with the fulfilment of resolve. This, contradicts truthfulness.

This is why God has said, *[Among the believers are] men who have been true to their covenant with God*.[32]

Anas [b. Mālik] related that his uncle Anas b. al-Naḍr was not present at the [battle of] Badr with the Messenger of God. This distressed [his uncle], who said, 'The first battlefield seen by the Messenger of God and I was absent from it. By God, if God should let me see a battlefield with His Messenger (God bless him and grant him peace), He will surely see what I would do.'

[Anas] said that he [his uncle] was present at the [Battle of] Uḥud the following year. Saʿd b. Muʿādh, who met him [on his way], asked him, 'Abū ʿUmar, whereto?'

'Happily, towards the sweet fragrance of Paradise, for I sense its fragrance this side of Uḥud.' He fought until he was slain. On his body, they found some eighty wounds from arrows, blows and stabbings.[33] His sister Bint al-Naḍr said, 'I recognised my brother only from his dress.' Then this verse [of the Qur'ān] was revealed, *[Among the believers] are men who have been true to their vow with God*.[34]

The Messenger of God stood by Musʿab b. ʿUmayr, who had

considered as a possible successor to the Prophet.

fallen at Uḥud as a martyr and who was the Messenger's standard-bearer. He recited, [*Among the believers*] *are men have been true to their vow with God, and among them are those who have passed on and others who are ready to fulfil their vow*.'[35]

Said Fuḍayl b. ᶜUbayd, 'I heard ᶜUmar b. al-Khaṭṭāb (may God be pleased with him) say that he heard God's Messenger say, "Martyrs consist of four [types of] men. [The first is] a believing man, excellent of faith, who encounters the enemy and is true to God until he is killed. On the Day of Resurrection, people shall raise their eyes to him in like fashion"—[the Messenger of God] raised his head until his headgear fell,' and, said the reporter, 'I could no longer see either ᶜUmar's or the Messenger's headgears.'

'"[The second type is] a man, excellent of faith, who meets the enemy and is hit perchance by an arrow, as if by the thorn of an acacia tree, and dies. His is the second degree.

'"[The third type is] the believing man who mixes the good deed with the bad. He meets up with the enemy and remains true to God until he is killed. His is the third degree.

'"[The fourth] is a believer who is dissipated, but, meeting the enemy, is true to God until he is killed. His is the fourth degree.'[36]

Said Mujāhid, 'Two men emerged from a crowd of seated people and said, "If God should bestow upon us money, we shall give alms."[37] But they were miserly with their money and it was revealed, *Among them are those who made covenant with God: If we are granted God's bounty, we shall give in charity and be among the righteous*.'[38] A man said, 'This is a thing they had intended inside themselves not to speak of,' and so God declare, *Among them are those who made covenant with God: If we are granted of God's bounty, we shall give in charity and be among the righteous. But when he gave them of His bounty, they became miserly with it and turned away disinclined. So, God punished them with hypocrisy in their hearts until the day they shall meet Him, because they broke their covenant and because they lied.*[39]

Thus, resolution is a promise: to break it is lying and to fulfil it is truthfulness. This truthfulness is stronger than the third kind of truthfulness. The soul may have abundant resolve but then temporises, from the difficulty of fulfilling it and from the tumult of passion upon consolidation and the procurement of means.

This is why God excluded ʿUmar, who said, 'Were I to be put forward, I prefer that my neck be struck than to govern a people with Abū Bakr [still] in their midst, O Lord, unless my soul entices me about something in killing which I do not find now. For I am not secure that this will weigh upon my soul to change its resolve.'[40] With this he bespoke the severity of the fulfilment of resolution.

Said Abū Saʿīd [Aḥmad b. ʿĪsā] al-Kharrāz,[A] 'I dreamed of two angels descended from Heaven. They asked me, "What is truthfulness?" "The fulfilment of promise," said I. "Truthful art thou," they said as they veered back to Heaven.'

The fifth type of truthfulness pertains to works—namely, that a person sees to it that his external works do not point to anything within him which is not ascribed to him. He does not forsake works but[41] makes the interior a confirmation of the exterior. This is the opposite of what we said on the [necessity of] forsaking ostentation, because the exhibitionist is one who aims [precisely] at this for the sake of people.[42] Many a person [also]

[A] Abū Saʿīd Aḥmad b. ʿĪsā al-Kharrāz (d. 899) hailed from Baghdad and authored the deeply influential *Kitāb al-ṣidq* (see Sulamī's *Ṭabaqāt al-ṣūfiya*, 228–32). He developed his themes around the concepts of 'interiority' and 'exteriority', 'proximity' and 'remoteness' from God, which led him to the first pronouncements recorded on *fanā'* (annihilation in God) and *baqā'* (subsistence in God). According to him, the wayfarer has to pass through the stations of fear, hope, trust, love, shame, longing and intimacy (Arberry's preface and translation, *The Book of Truthfulness*, vi). However, Kharrāz raises a crucial question about proximity and extinction,[see, Arberry, 'Preface,' *The Book of Truthfulness*, iv.] one that must have troubled many a jurist in his time—in Arberry's words, 'does the mystic reach a stage in which he ceases consciously to strive after truthfulness?' His answer poignantly refers to 'stations' that cannot be penned down for description. This view obviously draws in, among other things, language and its articulation and, of course, the Book and its relationship to creation—all questions of fundamental importance to the later Sufis and philosophers alike.

stands in prayer with the appearance of humility not intending this for the sake of being seen by others, while his heart is oblivious to the prayer. Anyone looking at him sees him standing before God, though in his interior he stands in the marketplace before one of his desires.

Those acts interpret the interior as the [actual] state in a manner that contains a falsehood, though we are asked to be truthful in our actions. Likewise, a man may walk with the appearance of serenity and dignity without his interior having any such dignified trait. This person is not truthful in his actions, even if he is unmindful of people or unostentatious before them. One is saved from this only when secrecy and openness are equal, when his interior is like or better than his exterior.[43]

Fearing this, some have chosen to obscure the exterior, cloaking themselves in the garment of the evildoers that no one may suppose anything better on account of their exterior. This belies how the exterior indicates the interior.

Therefore, whenever[44] the exterior is intended to contradict the interior, this is called ostentation, and it is a departure from sincerity.[45] But when the contradiction is inadvertent, it departs from truthfulness. This is why the Messenger of God (may God bless him and grant him peace) said, 'Lord, make me better in private than in public. And make me true in public.'[46]

Said Yazīd b. al-Ḥārith, 'If God's servant is the same in private as he is in public, that is justice. If he is better in private than public, that is merit. But if he is better in public than in private, that is injustice.' This is thrown into relief by:

When secrecy and avowal in the faithful one are equal,
    in both abodes he is esteemed, worthy of praise.
But if avowal belies secrecy—what has he
    in his pursuit of gain save toil and hardship?
As the[47] authentic *dinar* at the market is in demand
    so its counterfeit is refused, with not a weight-value to
    fetch.[48]

Said ʿAṭiyya[49] b. ʿAbd al-Ghāfir, 'When the private self of the faithful one agrees with his public self, God takes pride in him with the angels, saying, "This truly is my servant."'[50]

Said Muʿāwiya b. Qurra, 'Who will show me the one who weeps by night and smiles by day?'[51]

And said ʿAbd al-Wāḥid b. Zayd, 'Whenever al-Ḥasan [al-Baṣrī] was charged with anything, he acted upon it with more alacrity than other people. Whenever he was prohibited from anything he forsook it more effectually than other people. I have never seen anyone whose private self resembled more his public face than he.'[52]

Abū ʿAbd al-Raḥmān [Muḥammad b. al-Ḥusayn] al-Zāhid used to say, 'My God, in my dealings with people, I treated them with fidelity. But in my dealings with Thee, I treated Thee with betrayal'—and he wept.

Said Abū Yaʿqūb al-Nahrajūrī, 'Truthfulness is agreement with the truth in private and in public.'

Thus, the equivalence of the private[53] with the public is one kind of truthfulness.

The sixth type of truthfulness—the highest, most honourable level—is truthfulness[54] in the stations of religion; such as truthfulness in fear, hope, the glorification [of God], contentment, reliance [on Him], love[55] and other similar matters. These matters have beginnings, the appearance of which gives rise to the name; and they have goals and realities. The truthful person of attainment is he who has attained their realities. When he masters the thing and its reality is perfected, the person who possesses the thing is said to be truthful in it—as when one says, 'such-and-such a person is a true fighter', 'this is true fear' or 'that is true desire'.

Said God, *Only they are faithful who have faith in God and His Messenger, but have not then doubted...such are the truthful;*[56] *But it is the righteous one who has faith in God and the Last Day...such are the truthful.*[57] Asked about faith, Abū Dharr recited that verse of the Qur'ān. He was told that they had asked him about faith. He answered, 'I asked God's Messenger (may God bless him and grant him peace) about faith and he recited this verse.'[58]

We will take fear as an example. There is no servant who has faith in God and the Last Day who does not fear God so that the term is applied to him, although the fear may not be true—that is, it may not attain the level of a reality. Whereas fearing a ruler or highway robber during his travel, how his colour sometimes turns pale! Both his sides trembling, his life discomposed, he is incapable of either eating or sleeping—so smitten by thought that he becomes useless to either wife or children. He is incited away from his abode, exchanging amity for forlornness, tranquillity for trouble and hardship; and exposing himself to dangers. All this from fear of a perceived peril. He [claims] to fear the Fire; yet nothing of the above befalls him when he sins. This is why the Prophet said, 'I have seen nothing like the Fire, where the one fleeing it is fast asleep, and nothing like Paradise where the one seeking it is fast asleep.'[59]

Realising these things is very rare. The only purpose of these stations is their perfection. However, each of God's servants benefits according to his own state—either weak or strong. If his state is strong he is called truthful in it.

Knowing, glorifying and fearing God have no end. This is why the Prophet said to Gabriel, 'I long to see thee in thy proper form.' Gabriel replied: 'You are incapable of it.'

'No, show me!' he said.

So, Gabriel gave appointment for Baqīᶜ,[A] on a moonlit night, thus granting [his wish]. The Prophet looked on as [Gabriel] filled the entire horizon—meaning every corner of the heavens. The Prophet then fell over in a swoon.[60] He came to again and Gabriel had returned to his previous form. The Prophet said, 'I never thought any of God's creatures could be thus!'

He replied, 'What then if you had seen Isrāfīl? For the Throne sits upon his nape, his two legs penetrate downwards to the limits of the lower earth.[61] Yet, so diminutive was he before the glory of God that he was like a *waṣaᶜ*'—that is, like a small bird.'[62] Notice

[A] Baqīᶜ al-Gharad is the cemetery of Medina.

that however much he may be enveloped in exaltedness and awe, he is reduced to that limit. The other angels are not like this because they differ in knowledge. This indeed is truthfulness in glorification.

Said Jābir [bin ᶜAbd Allāh al-Anṣārī], 'The Messenger of God (may God bless him and grant him peace) has said, "On the Night of the Ascension,[A] I passed by Gabriel at the supreme Heaven and he was like a threadbare saddle-blanket from fear of God (Exalted is He)"'—that is to say, like the cover thrown over the back of the camel.[63]

Similarly, the Companions used to be fearful. But they had not attained the same fear as that of God's Messenger. This is why Ibn ᶜUmar said about it, 'You will not attain the reality of faith before you come to regard all people as foolish in God's religion.'[64]

Said Muṭarrif [b. ᶜAbd Allāh b. al-Shikhkhīr al-Baṣrī], 'There is not a person who is not foolish in respect of what is between him and his Lord; save that one fool is more contemptible than the other.'[65]

Said the Prophet, 'The servant will attain to the reality of faith only when he sees people like camels at God's side.[B] Then, turning back to his own self, he finds it baser than the base.'[66]

The truthful person at all these stations is rare.[67] The degrees of truthfulncss arc without end. The servant of God may be truthful in one thing but not another; if he is truthful in everything, he is indeed the perfectly truthful.

Said Saᶜd b. Muᶜādh [b. al-Nuᶜmān], 'I am strong in three things and weak in everything else. Since I have embraced Islam, never

[A] I.e., *laylat al-miᶜrāj*.

[B] The sacred texts of Islam use different imageries to describe God's attributes, such as that of the King. While camels were used almost everywhere in the medieval world, the camel imagery suggests both the dependence of beasts of burden on the master as they carry out his commands, on the on hand, *and* the master's protection of his precious herd, on the other. This clearly indicates well old Arabia's value system, where camels were more than just wealth.

have I pondered anything while performing a prayer, but only once I was done with praying. Never have I attended a funeral[68] where I pondered what the deceased had said and what utterance is ascribed to him until we were done with his burial.[69] Finally, I have never listened to anything uttered by God's Messenger (may God bless him and grant him peace) but that I knew it to be the truth.' Said Ibn al-Musayyib, 'I did not know that these character traits were found together in any but the Prophet (may God bless him and grant him peace).'[70]

Therefore, this is [what] truthful [means] in these matters. How people among the eminent Companions performed prayers and took part in funerals without attaining this scope![A] These then are the levels and meanings of truthfulness. Most cases of the reported sayings of the masters on the reality of truthfulness pertain only to one or another of these meanings.

Abū Bakr al-Warrāq did indeed assert that truthfulness is of three [kinds]: truthfulness in Divine unity, truthfulness in obedience and truthfulness in knowledge. The truthfulness of Divine unity is incumbent on all the faithful. God said, [*The believers*] *who are faithful to God and His Messenger...these are the truthful.*[71] The truthfulness of obedience is incumbent on people of learning and devoutness. The truthfulness of knowledge is incumbent on those possessed of sainthood (*walāya*) and who are the mainstays of this earth.[72]

All this has to do with what we said in connection with the sixth type of truthfulness. While this indicates the aspects found in truthfulness, it does not include all aspects.

Jaʿfar al-Ṣādiq said that truthfulness is struggle and never choosing anything else besides God, just as He chooses nothing else but you for God has said, *He has selected you.*[73]

It is said[74] that God inspired Moses (God grant him peace) thus: 'When I love a servant I afflict him with trials which mountains

[A] Implying that such a level of truthfulness sometimes eluded the Companions too.

cannot withstand, that I may see how he is truthful. If I find him patient, I take him as My friend and dear one. When I find him restless, complaining about Me to people, untroubled I leave him.'[75]

Therefore, one of the signs of truthfulness is silence in both adversity and pious works, and an aversion to the popular understanding of this. But God knows best.

NOTES

[Prologue]

1 Q. XCVIII.4.

2 Q. XXV.25.

Chapter 1

1 Q. VI.52.

2 A, 155: '*wa li-kull*'; B, 5: '*wa innamā li-kull*'.

3 Bukhārī, *Imān*, I:2, no. 1; Muslim, *Imāra*, III:33, no. 155; Ibn Ḥanbal I:25; Ibn Māja, *K. al-zuhd*, II:1413, no. 4227.

4 Ibn Ḥanbal I:397.

5 Q. IV.35.

6 Muslim, *K. al-Birr*, 292, no. 33; Ibn Māja, *K. al-zuhd*, 1388, no. 4143; Ibn Ḥanbal II:285, 539; cf. Zabīdī 6; *Qūt* II:160.

7 Qūt II:160; cf. Zabīdī 6.

8 Qūt II:160.

9 *Ibid.*

10 A, 156: '*yabtaghī*'; B, 7: '*li-yabtaghī*'.

11 *Qūt* II:161.

12 *Qūt* II:161.

13 *Ibid.*

14 *Ibid.*

15 *Ibid.*

16 *Ibid.*; Muslim, *K. al-Imān*, I:125, nos. 203, 204, 206–7, 209; Ibn Ḥanbal I:227, 2:234, 3:149.

17 Ibn Māja, *K. al-zuhd*, II:1375, no. 4105; Qūt II:161.

18 Ibn Ḥanbal III:311, 319, 338, 371; *Qūt* II:161; cf. Irāqī 157.

19 *Qūt* II:161.

20 *Ibid.*

21 *Ibid.*

22 Bukhārī, *Īmān*, I:35, no. 30; *Diyāt*, IX:6, no. 14; Muslim, *Qisāma*, III:164, no. 33; *al-Fitan wa-ashrāṭ al-sāʿa*, IV:520, nos. 14–5; Ibn Māja, *Fitan*, II:1311, nos. 3963–64; *Qūt* II:161.

23 Cf. Ibn Māja, *Nikāḥ*, I:607, nos. 1886–87; *Qūt* II:161.

24 Cf. Ibn Ḥanbal II:112; Zabīdī 10–1; *Qūt* II:162.

25 *Qūt* II:158.

26 Cf. Ibn Ḥanbal V:446.

27 *Qūt* II:159.

28 *Ibid.*

29 *Ibid.* Instead of 'just as well as they learned *to act*', Makkī wrote 'just as well as they learned *knowledge*.'

30 *Ibid.*, II:159.

31 A, 158: '*yaʿṭī*'; B, 12: '*taʿṭī*'.

32 *Qūt* II:159.

33 *Ibid.*

34 *Ibid.*

35 With variation: Muslim, *Fitan*, IV:517, n. 8; Ibn Māja, *Zuhd*, II:1414, nos. 4229–30.

36 Q. XLVII.31.

37 A, 159: '*faḍaḥtunā*'; B, 12: '*afaḍaḥtunā*'.

38 *Qūt* II:160.

39 This entire sentence is missing in B.

40 A, 159: '*ḥattā yanẓur fī ʿamalihi, fa-idhā ʿamala lam yadaʿhu Allāh ḥattā yanẓur fī waraʿihi, fa-in tawarraʿ lam yadaʿhu*'; all missing in B.

41 Ibn Māja, *Zuhd*, II:1413, no. 4227.

Chapter 2

1 A, 160: '*intaḍat*'; B, 13: '*intahat*'.

2 A, 160: '*khādima*'; B, 13: '*ḥāditha*'.

3 A, 161: '*wa annahu lawlā*'; B, 14: '*lawlā*'.

4 A, 161: '*li-gharaḍ*'; B, 14: '*gharaḍ*'.

5 A, 161: '*law*'; B, 15: '*lawmā*'.

6 A, 161: '*takhfīfihi*'; B, 15: '*taḥqīqihi*'.

7 Ibn Māja, *Zuhd*, II:1413, n. 4227.

Chapter 3

1 *Qūt* II:159.

2 A, 162: '*al-niyya*'; B, 16: '*al-niyya al-muttaṣila*'.

3 A, 163: '*ya'nas bi-rabbihi*'; B, 17: '*ya'nas*'.

4 A, 163: '*taqwā*'; B, 17: '*yaqwā*'.

5 A, 163: '*bil-ʿilm*'; B, 17: '*bil-mayl*'.

6 A, 163: 'ʿasar'; B, 17: '*taʿsur*'.

7 A, 163: '*al-muḥāwara ta'akkada mayluhu*'; B, 17: '*al-mujāwara*'.

8 A, 163: '*al-dunyā lā al-ākhira*'; B, 17: '*al-dunyā lil-dunyā lā lil-ākhira*'.

9 A, 163: '*al-ṭaʿa*'; B, 17: '*al-ṭāʿāt*'.

10 Bukhārī, *Imān*, II:35–6, no. 51; Ibn Māja, *Fitan*, II:1318–19, no. 3984.

11 Q. XXII.37.

12 A, 164: '*al-mayl ilayhi*'; B, 18: '*al-mayl*'.

13 A, 164: '*tadāwī*'; B, 18: '*yadāwī*'.

14 A, 164: '*istakāna*'; B, 18: '*istaʿāna*'.

15 Ibn Ḥanbal II:263, 387.

16 *Qūt* II:161; cf. Zabīdī 8, 18.

17 Qūt II:160.

Chapter 4

1 Ibn Māja, *Muqaddamah*, I:81, no. 224; cf. Tirmidhī, *ʿilm*, IV:137–38, nos. 2784–85.

2 A, 166: '*ḥuẓūẓ al-nafs*'; B, 20: '*ḥuẓūẓ al-nufūs*'.

3 *Qūt* II:153.

4 A, 166: '*fa-kayfa*'; B, 20: '*fa-yukayyif*'.

5 Q. XXI.7.

6 *Qūt* II:153.

7 A, 167: '*al-khayl wal-ribāṭ*'; B, 22: '*al-khayl*'.

8 A, 167: '*lā an*'; B, 22: '*lā fī an*'.

9 A, 167: '*bi-anna*'; B, 22: '*fa-inna*'.

10 A, 167: '*mā taʿawwadhū*'; B, 22: '*lam yataʿawwadhū*'.

11 Zabīdī 22.

12 A, 168: '*maʿṣiya bil-qaṣd*'; B, 23: '*maʿṣiya*'.

13 A, 168: '*wa huwa annahu idhā*'; B, 23: '*wa huwa annahu*'.

14 *Iḥyā*, vol. III, Bk 31.

15 *Qūt* II:154. A, 168: '*al-taḍāᶜuf*'; B, 23: '*thumma al-taḍāᶜuf*'.

16 A, 168: '*yablagh*'; B, 23: '*tablagh*'.

17 Ibn Ḥanbal VI:136.

18 Cf. Zabīdī 23.

19 Q. III.200.

20 Zabīdī 23.

21 Thought to be one of Kaᶜb al-Aḥbar's sayings (Zabīdī 24).

22 Muslim, *Zakāt*, II:127, no. 55; Tirmidhī, *Abwāb al-barr wal-ṣilah*, III:216, no. 1986.

23 This is a reference to Muslim III:310, ns. 98–9.

24 A, 169: '*ḥayā'*'; B, 24: '*khashyatan*'.

25 A, 169: '*tadull*'; B, 24: '*tadulluhu*'.

26 Zabīdī 24. For another version of the 'seven traits', see Abū Jaᶜfar Muḥammad b. ᶜAlī b. al-Ḥusayn b. Bābawayh, *Kitāb al-khisāl*, 402–3.

27 A, 170: '*al-khatarāt wal-khatawāt*'; B, 25: '*al-khatawāt wal-khatarāt*'.

28 A, 170: '*yashābuh*'; B, 25: '*tashābuh*'.

29 Zabīdī 25.

30 *Qūt* II:162.

31 *Ibid.*; cf. Ibn Ḥanbal II:112 and Zabīdī 10–1.

32 A, 170: '*li-yaḥsuduh*'; B, 75: '*li-taḥsuduh*'.

33 Muslim, *Jannah*, IV:511, n. 79; Tirmidhī, *Abwāb ṣifat al-qiyāmah*, IV:40, no. 2543.

34 Ibn Māja, *Iqāmat al-ṣalāt wal-sunnah fī-hā*, I:349, nos. 1097–98; Ibn Ḥanbal V:420; cf. Bukhārī, *Jumᶜah*, II:30, nos. 5, 8, 10.

35 Q. VI.108.

36 *Qūt* II:154.

37 A, 171: '*wa taṭyīb*'; B, 26: '*wa min al-inbiṣāṭ taṭyīb*'.

38 A, 172: '*al-wiqāᶜ*'; B, 27: '*al-nikāḥ*'.

39 A, 172: '*li-dhālika*'; B, 27: '*ka-dhālika*'.

40 A, 172: '*ghayrahu lahu*'; B, 27: '*ghayrahu*'.

41 *Qūt* II:153.

42 *Ibid.*

43 Q. L.18.

44 A, 172: '*fa-taribtuh*'; B, 28: '*fa-atrabtuh*'.

45 *Qūt* II:163.

46 Reference unavailable.

47 *Ibid.*, II:152; Qushayrī, *Risāla*, '*Ikhlāṣ*' 163.

48 A, 173: '*al-dāᶜī*'; B, 28: '*li-dāᶜī*'.

49 A, 173: '*takharraj min ḥayyiz ahl al-ightirār*'; missing in B.

50 A, 173: '*lahu*'; B, 28: '*ilayhi*'.

51 *Qūt* II:156.

52 Although Ghazālī meant Sufyān al-Thawrī, Zabīdī disputes this and suggest Thaqafī instead (cf. Zabīdī 29).

53 *Ibid.*

54 *Ibid.*, II:152.16ff.

Chapter 5

1 A, 174: '*wa fikr*'; B, 29: '*aw fikr*'.

2 A, 174: '*min jamīᶜ*'; B, 29: 'ᶜ*an jamīᶜ*'.

3 A, 174: '*fadlahā*'; B, 30: '*fadlahu*'.

4 A, 174: '*bil-sharᶜ*'; B, 30: '*ayy bil-llāh wal-yawm wal-ākhira wa mā aᶜaddahu*'.

5 A, 174: '*li-hādhā*'; B, 20: '*li-dhā*'.

6 *Qūt* II:152.

7 *Ibid.*, II:163.

8 A, 175: 'Ḥammād b. Sulaymān'; B, 31: 'Ḥammād b. Abī Sulaymān'.

9 *Qūt* II:152.

10 A, 175: '*yaqūl*'; B, 21: '*fa-qāl*'. *Qūt* II:163.

11 Reference unidentified.

12 Cf. Zabīdī 31.

13 A, 175: '*fa-intafaʿtu*'; B, 31: '*fa-intafaʿtu bihi*'.

14 *Qūt* II:152.

15 Ibn Mubārak, *K. al-Zuhd* 1118, no. 240.

16 Reference unidentified.

17 Reference unidentified.

18 A, 175: '*bi-lisānih*'; B, 31: '*bi-qalbih*'.

19 A, 175: '*ḍaʿīfa*'; B, 32: '*ḍaʿīfa lā maska lahā*'.

20 A, 175: '*tatasayyar*'; B, 32: '*yatayassar*'.

21 A, 176: '*yaʿizz ʿalā basīṭ al-arḍ man yafhamuhā*'; B, 32: '*yaʿizz man yafhamuhā*'.

22 A, 176: '*tujāwiz*'; B, 32: '*yujāwiz*'.

23 Q. VI.52.

24 Q. XLIV.54.

25 A, 176: '*kamā yusakhkhir al-mutanaʿʿim bil-naẓar ilā al-ḥūr al-ʿīn miman yatanaʿʿam bil-naẓar ilā wajh al-ṣuwar*'; B, 32: '*ka-man yatanaʿʿam bil-naẓar ilā wajh al-ṣuwar*'.

26 A, 176: '*iʿrāḍuhum*'; B, 32: '*iʿrāḍuhā*'.

27 A, 176: '*annahā*'; B, 32: '*annahu*'.

28 Q. XI.118.

29 Q. XXX.32.

30 Q. XI.119.

31 Zabīdī 33. A, 176: '*yaṭlubūnā minnī al-janna*'; B, 33: '*yaṭlubbūna minnī*'.

32 A, 176: '*wa raʾā*'; B, 33: '*wa yaḥkī raʾā*'.

33 Qushayrī, *Risāla* 608.

34 *Ibid.*, 610.

35 A, 176: '*wa taʿālā ilayya*'; B, 33: '*wa taʿālā*'. See Zabīdī 33.

36 A, 177: '*lā yataʿayyar*'; B, 33: '*lam yatayassar*'.

37 *Qūt* II:153.

38 A, 177: '*yataqawwā*'; B, 33: '*yaqwā*'.

39 *Qūt* II:153.

Chapter 6

1 Q. XCVIII.5.

2 Q. XXXIX.3.

3 Q. IV.146.

4 Q. XVIII.110.

5 Qurayshī, *Risāla* 162. The rest of the tradition reads: 'and its perfection, the admonition of leaders about the affairs and the need for the community of Muslims.'

6 Zabīdī 43–5.

7 Cf. *Qūt* II:159.

8 Cf. Zabīdī 45.

9 Muslim, *Imāra*, III:374–75, no. 152 (with some variation).

10 A, 180: '*faṣala*'; B, 46: '*yafṣil*'.

11 A, 180: '*tashbaʿ*'; B, 46: '*tattasiʿ*'.

12 A, 180: '*makānahā*'; B, 46: '*makānahā ukhrā*'.

13 A, 180: '*mā dhakarahu*'; B, 46: '*mā dhakarahu liya*'.

14 *Qūt* II:162.

15 Q. XV.40.

16 A, 181: '*Sulaymān*'; B, 47: '*Abū Sulaymān*'.

17 Cf. *Qūt* II: 156.

18 *Ibid.*, II:159; cf. Zabīdī 47.

19 *Qūt* II:159.

20 *Ibid.*

21 Shaʿrānī, *al-Ṭabaqāt al-kubrā* I (Cairo, 1317), 29.

22 *Qūt* II:151.

23 Cf. Zabīdī 48.

24 Reference to Q. XVI.66; cf. *Qūt* II:159.

25 Ghazālī mistakenly gives him 'al-Tustarī' for *nisba* (from Syria). In his *Risāla*, Qushayrī describes him as one of the ancient learned and a friend of Abū Turāb al-Nakhashī (Zabīdī 48); (cf. *Qūt* II:152, where Makkī committed the same mistake).

26 *Qūt* II:154.

27 A, 182: '*kharaja*'; B, 48: '*uktub kharaja*'.

28 *Qūt* II:155.

29 *Ibid.*, II:163

30 Reference unidentified.

31 Reference unidentified.

32 Reference unidentified.

33 This last sentence does not appear in A, 182.

Chapter 7

1 Q. XVI.66.

2 A, 183: '*wāḥid ʿalā al-tajarrud*'; B, 50: '*wāḥid*'.

3 A, 183: 'ʿanhu'; B, 50: '*minhu*'.

4 A, 183: '*qad dhakarnā*'; B, 50: '*dhakaranā*'.

5 *Iḥyā'*, 962–91 [from the 2nd edition containing the whole *Ihya'*: Beirut: Dār al-Kutub al-ʿilmiyya, 2011].

6 A, 183: 'ʿan'; B, 50: '*min*'.

7 A, 183: '*yaqdir bihi*'; B, 50: '*maqdaratahu bihi*'.

8 A, 183: '*li-yakūna*'; B, 50: '*yakūna*'.

9 A, 184: '*tataṭarraq*'; B, 51: '*taṭarraq*'.

10 Muslim IV:595, no. 46; Ibn Māja, *Zuhd*, II:1405, no. 4202–3.

11 Reference unidentified.

12 A, 184: '*al-niya*'; B, 51: '*bayān al-niya*'.

13 A, 185: 'ʿan'; B, 52: 'ʿanhu'.

14 A, 185: '*ḥaythu*'; B, 52: '*idh*'.

15 A, 185: '*qill*'; B, 52: '*qallamā*'.

16 Q. XXXIX.47–9.

17 Q. XVIII:103–4.

18 A, 186: '*afḍal*'; B, 53: '*lil-afḍal*'.

19 A, 186: '*bi-taṣaddī*'; B, 53: '*li-taṣaddī*'.

20 A, 186: '*li-anna*'; B, 53: '*idhā*'.

21 Q. XXXVIII.83.

Chapter 8

1 A, 186: '*ilā ikhlāṣ*'; B, 54: '*ilā al-ikhlāṣ*'.

2 Cf. *Qūt* II:154.:151, 159.

3 Reference unidentified.

4 Zabīdī 54.

5 Qushayrī, *Risāla* 362.

6 A, 187: '*wajh*'; B, 55: '*huwa wajh*'.

7 A, 187: '*huwa al-qā'il*'; B, 55: '*qawl al-qā'il*'.

8 A, 187: 'ʿammā'; B, 55: '*mimmā*'.

9 Zabīdī 55.

10 A, 187: '*yaʿmal*'; B, 56: '*yaʿmal al-ʿamal*'.

11 *Qūt* II:156.

12 Reference unidentified.

13 Qushayrī, *Risāla* 15, 163.

14 Reference unidentified.

15 Ibn Māja, *Fitan*, II:1314, no. 3972, with variation.

Chapter 9

1 A, 189: '*yaʿlam an*'; B, 58: '*yaʿlam ayḍan an*'.

2 A, 189: '*baynuhu*'; B, 58: '*baynahumā*'.

3 B, 52, : '*jamīʿan*'.

4 This entire sentence is missing in B, 58.

5 A, 189: '*tafaṭṭana*'; B, 58: '*yafṭan*'.

6 A, 190: '*al-khalwa wa lākin lā yakhtaṣṣ*'; B, 58: '*al-khalwa wa murāqabat al-qalb fī dūn waqt lā yujdī nafʿan law lā an tadūm fī al-aḥwāl kullihā wa lākin yakhtaṣṣ*'.

7 Ibn Ḥanbal III:28; cf. *K. al-ʿilm, K. dhamm al-jāh wa'l-riyā'*.

8 A, 190: '*lil-mutashammirīn*'; B, 59: '*lil-mushammirīn*'.

9 A, 190: '*yadʿūhu*'; B, 59: '*yadʿu*'.

10 A, 190: 'ʿan hādhihi'; B, 59: '*min hādhihi*'.

11 A, 190: '*bi-ḥusn ṣūrah*'; B, 59: '*ṣūrah*'.

12 A, 190: '*al-waḍʿayn*'; B, 59: '*al-waṣfayn*'.

13 Zabīdī 59.

14 A, 191: '*al-nāqid al-baṣīr*'; B, 59: '*al-nāqid*'.

15 A, 191: '*amr*'; B, 59: '*ahl*'.

Chapter 10

1 A, 191: '*ikhtalafa al-nāss*'; B, 60: '*ikhtalafa*'.

2 A, 191: '*al-bāʿith*'; B, 61: '*al-bawāʿith*'.

3 A, 191: '*mufḍī lil-ʿiqāb*'; B, 60: '*muqtaḍī*'.

4 Q. XCIX.7–8.

5 Q. IV.40.

6 A, 192: '*yaḍurruhu*'; B, 61: '*yaḍurru*'.

7 A, 192: '*bi-mā*'; B, 61: '*mā*'.

8 A, 192: '*yubʿiduhu*'; B, 61: '*yubʿiduhu shibran*'.

9 Reference unidentified.

10 A, 192: '*fa-idhā*'; B, 62: '*fa-in*'.

11 A, 192: '*al-maḥḍ*'; B, 62: '*al-riyā' al-maḥḍ*'.

12 A, 192: '*al-tābiʿ*'; B, 62: '*wa'l-safar al-tābiʿ*'.

13 Others like Mujāhid and Saʿīd b. Jubayr (Zabīdī 62). A, 193: '*wa ghayruhu*'; B, 62: '*wa ʿidda*'.

14 Q. XVIII.110.

15 Reference unidentified.

16 Reference unidentified.

17 Ibn Māja, *Zuhd*, II:1406, no. 4203.

18 A, 193: '*ʿamalan liya*'; B, 63: '*ʿamalan*'.

19 Muslim IV:595, no. 46; Ibn Māja, *Zuhd*, II:1405, no. 4202–3.

20 Ibn Māja, *Jihād*, II:931, no. 2783.

21 *Lisān al-ʿArab* X:375.

22 A, 194: 'ʿanhu qāla'; B, 63: '*qāla*'.

23 Bukhārī, *Imān*, I:2, no. 1; Muslim, *Imāra*, III:33, no. 155; Ibn Ḥanbal I:25; Ibn Māja, *K. al-zuhd*, II:1413, no. 4227.

24 A, 194: '*inna al-insān*'; B, 63: '*al-insān*'.

25 Q. XVIII.110.

26 A, 194: '*wa in lam*'; B, 63: '*wa lam*'.

27 A, 194: '*lā thawāb*'; B, 63: '*innahu lā thawāb*'.

28 A, 195: '*Rawwād*'; B, 64: '*Dā'ūd*'.

29 Zabīdī 64.

30 A, 195: '*al-āfa wa'l-riyā*''; B, 65: '*al-āfa*'.

31 A, 195: '*fī al-ikhlāṣṣ yawman*'; B, 64: '*yawman fī al-ikhlāṣṣ*'.

32 A, 195: '*idh*'; B, 64: '*inna*'.

33 *Qūt* II:163.

34 *Ibid.*, II:151, 159; cf. Q. CXII.

Chapter 11

1 Q. XXXIII.23.

2 A, 195: '*al-fujūr*'; B, 68: '*imma al-fujūr*'.

3 Muslim IV:317–8, nos. 103–5; Ibn Māja, *Muqaddama*, I:18, no. 46; cf. Bukhārī, *Adab*, VIII:46, no. 120.

4 Q. XIX.41.

5 Q. XIX.54. This quotation is missing in B, 69.

6 Q. XIX.56.

7 Cf. Zabīdī 69.

8 Reference unidentified.

9 Reference unidentified.

10 A, 196: '*al-ḥaqq*'; B, 69: '*al-waqt*'.

11 Reference unidentified.

12 A, 196: '*ṣidqan*'; B, 69: '*ṣādiqan*'.

13 Reference unidentified.

14 Reference unidentified.

15 Q. XXXIX:60.

16 A, 196: '*al-Thawrī*'; B, 69: '*al-Nūrī*'.

17 Reference unidentified.

18 A, 196: '*fī al-ʿalāniyya*'; missing in B, 69. Qushayri, *Risāla* 378.

19 Allusion to Q. II.50. Reference unidentified.

20 Reference unidentified.

21 A, 196: '*awfā*'; B, 70: '*awfar*'.

22 Reference unidentified.

23 A, 197: 'ātāka'; B, B, 70: '*afāduka*'.

24 Reference unidentified.

25 Zabīdī 7.

26 A, 197: '*min al-dhunūb*'; B, 70: '*mudhabdhibīn*'.

27 Reference unidentified.

28 Reference unidentified.

29 Reference unidentified.

30 Q. XXXIII.8.

31 Zabīdī 71.

Chapter 12

1 A, 197: '*fa-man*'; B, 72: '*wa man*'.

2 A, 198: '*wa lākin*'; missing in B, 72.

3 A, 198: '*aḥaduhumā*'; missing in B, 72.

4 Reference unidentified.

5 A, 198: '*ilayhi al-ḥāja*'; B, 72: '*al-ḥāja*'.

6 A, 198: '*wa fī al-hidhr ʿan*'; B, 72: '*wa hidhr min*'.

7 A, 198: '*kayy*'; B, 73: '*li-kaylā*'.

8 Zabīdī 73.

9 A, 199: '*afhama al-ẓālim*'; B, 73: '*afhama*'.

10 Q. VI.79.

11 A, 199: '*kidhb*'; B, 74: '*kādhib*'.

12 Q. I.5. A, 199: '*iyyāka naᶜbudu*'; B, 74: '*iyyāka naᶜbudu wa iyyaka nastaᶜīn*'.

13 Q. XIX.30.

14 A, 199: '*mā taqayyada*'; B, 75: '*mā taᶜabbada*'.

15 Reference unidentified.

16 Ibn Māja, *Zuhd*, II:1385, nos. 4135–36.

17 A, 199: '*taqayyada*'; B, 75: '*taᶜabbada*'.

18 A, 199: '*huwa*'; B, 75; '*huwa huwa*'.

19 A, 199: '*wa hādhā*'; B, 75: '*fa-hādhā*'.

20 A, 199: '*iᶜtirāḍ* '; B, 75: '*iᶜrāḍ* '.

21 Zabīdī 75.

22 A, 200: '*kādhiban* '; B, 76: '*ṣādiqan* '.

23 Muslim, III:374, no. 152. *Supra*, p. 31, n. 168.

24 *Qūt* II:160.

25 Q. LXIII.1.

26 A, 200: '*an yaᶜtaqid*'; B, 76: '*annahu yaᶜtaqid*'.

27 A, 200: '*yuqaddum*'; B, 76: '*yuqaddim ᶜalā*'.

28 A, 200: '*hādhā*'; B, 76: '*li-hādhā*'.

29 A, 200: '*quwwa*'; B, 76: '*qawiyya*'.

30 For the traditions relating to the Saqīfa gathering, see *Ta'rīkh Ṭabarī* II:234.

31 A, 201: '*humm aw*'; B, 77: '*huwa wa*'.

32 Q. XXXIII.23.

33 A, 201: '*mā bayna*'; B, 77: '*min bayna*'.

34 Q. XXXIII.23. Zabīdī 78.

35 *Ibid.*, 79.

36 Reference unidentified.

37 A, 202: '*la-naṣaddaqanna*'; B, 79: '*la-naṣaddaqanna bihi*'.

38 Q. IX.75. Cf. Zabīdī 79.

39 Q. IX.75–7. Cf. Zabīdī 79.

40 Cf. Zabīdī 77.

41 A, 202: '*wa lākin*'; B, 80: '*wa dhālika*'.

42 A, 202: '*dhālika*'; B, 80: '*dhālika li-ajal al-khalq*'.

43 A, 203: '*min ẓāhirihi*'; B, 80: '*minhu*'.

44 A, 203: '*in kānat...summiyat*'; B, 80: '*in kāna...summiya*'.

45 A, 203: '*bihā*'; B, 80: '*bihi*'.

46 Tirmidhī, *Daᶜawāt*, V:231, no. 3656.

47 A, 203: '*fa-mā*'; B, 80: '*ka-mā*'.

48 Reference unidentified.

49 A, 203: 'ᶜAṭiyya'; B, 81: 'ᶜUqba '. The correct name is ᶜUqba b. ᶜAbd al-Ghāfir or Abū Nahār al-Awdī al-ᶜAwdhī al-Baṣrī (Zabīdī 81).

50 Reference unidentified.

51 Zabīdī 81.

52 *Ibid.*, 81.

53 A, 203: '*sarīra* '; B, 81: '*al-sirr*'.

54 A, 203: '*ṣidq*'; B, 81: '*wa huwa al-ṣidq*'.

55 A, 204: '*al-tawakkul wal-ḥubb*'; B, 81: '*al-tawakkul*'.

56 Q. XLIX.15.

57 Q. II.177.

58 Zabīdī 82.

59 Reference unidentified.

60 A, 205: '*huwa bihi*'; B, 82: '*huwa*'.

61 A, 205: '*al-arḍ* '; B, 82: '*al-arḍayn*'.

62 Ibn Ḥanbal v:59.

63 Zabīdī 83.

64 *Ibid.*, 83.

65 *Ibid.*

66 *Ibid.*

67 A, 205: '*jamīʿ hādhihi*'; B, 83: '*jamīʿ*'.

68 A, 205: '*wa lā shuyyiʿat*'; B, 83: '*wa mā shuyyiʿat*'.

69 A, 205: '*yafrugh*'; B, 83: '*nafrugh*'.

70 Reference unidentified.

71 Q. XLIX.15.

72 Reference unidentified.

73 Q. XX.78.

74 A, 206: '*wa qīla*'; B, 84: '*wa qad*'.

75 Reference unidentified.

APPENDIX

PERSONS CITED IN TEXT — EXCLUDING PROPHETS

ᶜABD ALLĀH B. ᶜUMAR B. AL-KHAṬṬĀB [d. 73/693]—Still young during the Prophet's lifetime, he nevertheless transmitted a large number of traditions. His moral strength earned him a reputation for fearlessness. While remaining aloof of political intrigues, he did not shrink from publicly rebuking al-Ḥajjāj b. Yūsuf (d. 714), governor and Caliph ᶜAbd al-Malik's lieutenant. [Abū Nuᶜaym I:292–314; Azmi 45]

ᶜABD AL-ᶜAZĪZ B. ABĪ DĀ'ŪD [d. 159/775–76]. Traditionist who died in Mecca. He was accused of espousing the doctrine of *irjāᶜ* (equivalent to laxism on the question of moral acts). [Abu Nuᶜaym VIII.191–203; Dhahabī (1) I.178; Ibn Ḥajar (2) I.604, no. 4110]

ᶜABD AL-WĀḤID B. ZAYD AL-BAṢRĪ [d. 177/193]. Ascetic from Basra known especially for his edifying preaching. [Abū Nuᶜaym VI.155–65; Ibn al-Jawzī III.240–44; Massignon, *Essai*, 213–215]

ABŪ ᶜABD AL-RAḤMĀN [MUḤAMMAD B. AL-ḤUSAYN] AL-ZĀHID. Unidentified.

ABŪ BAKR AL-BAQILLĀNĪ, QĀḌĪ [d. 403/1013]. The famous *mutakallim* of the Ashᶜarite persuasion.

ABŪ BAKR MUḤAMMAD B. ᶜUMAR AL-WARRĀQ AL-TIRMIDHĪ [240/854–55]. Mystic from Tirmidh and disciple of Aḥmad b. Khiḍrawayh. He lived in Balkh, where he was highly regarded. His writings earned him the title 'teacher of the saints'. [Sulamī 221–27]

ABŪ BAKR AL-SHIBLĪ, [d. 334/946]. Mystic from Baghdad. He adopted Sufism after working for a period as administrator. He was known for his verses and *shaṭaḥāt* (ecstatic states), and knew al-Ḥallāj. [Abū Nuᶜaym X:336–75; Ibn Jawzī II:258–60; Ibn Khallikān II:273–76; Sulamī 337–48]

ABŪ BAKR AL-ṢIDDĪQ, ibn Abī Quḥāfa al-Taymī [d. 13/634]. A close, early Companion of the Prophet and first caliph (*r.* 11/632–13/634). From Mecca he fled with the Prophet to Medina, where he continued as a major pillar of the nascent

Muslim community. Sufis tend to associate him with contemplative life. [Ibn Ḥanbal, *K. al-zuhd* 13–9; Nabhānī 1.127–28; Hujwīrī 97–9; *EI*^{2} 1.109–11]

ABŪ BAKR AL-WARRĀQ. Unidentified.

ABŪ BAKRA [51 or 52/671–2]—Literally, Man of the Pulley, a title given an Abyssinian Companion of the Prophet's named Nufayʿ b. Masrūḥ. While still enslaved by the Thaqafites, he used a pulley for a daring escape during the Muslim siege of Ṭā'if in order to join the side of the Prophet, who emancipated him. He stayed for some time in Yemen before taking part in the founding of Baṣra, where he finally settled. Abū Bakra kept his distance (*iʿtazala*) from conflicts involving the succession, including the Battle of the Camel, and worked on the estates bestowed on him by ʿUmar. *Ḥadīth* scholars regarded him as a trustworthy transmitter of traditions, and he left many descendants. At a time when an 'Arab' aristocracy was fighting to maintain its secular domination over other, newly converted ethnicities, al-Mahdī's refusal from the throne to recognize his descendants' new genealogical links with the clans ruined their claim to any other status but the Prophet's *mawālī*s. One famous descendant of his was Qāḍī Abū Bakra Bakkār b. Qutayba. [cf. Ibn Khallikān, no. 115; *EI*^{2} online]

ABŪ AL-DARDĀ', ʿUwaymir al-Khazrajī [d. 32/652]. A well-respected legal authority whom ʿUmar once sent as a teacher, with Ibn Masʿūd, to Kufa and Damascus. As an ascetic he advocated meditation and privileged the fear of God to mechanical ritual. He taught that a person obtained nothing from God before renouncing the world. Died in Damascus. [Ibn Ḥanbal 55–65; Massignon, *Essai* 158]

ABŪ DHARR, Jundab b. Junāda al-Ghifārī [32 or 33/652–654]. One of the first to embrace Islam, Abū Dharr transmitted many traditions incorporated in the collections of Bukhārī and Muslim, many of them on poverty. For later generations, he stood as the prototype of the *faqīr*. [Ibn Ḥanbal, *K. al-zuhd* 77–9; Abū Nuʿaym 1.156; Massignon 158–9; Schimmel 28; *EI*^{2} 1.118]

ABŪ HURAYRA, al-Dawsī al-Yamānī [d. 59/677]. Transmitted the largest number of traditions. He joined the Prophet at Khaybar, accompanying him for three or four years. Some authors, notably Abū Rayyah, alleged that he later favoured the Umayyads. Abū Hurayra lived mostly in Medina, where he died. [Abū Nuʿaym 1.376–85; Azmi 35–8; *EI*^{2} 1.132–33]

ABŪ MŪSĀ ʿABD ALLĀH B. QAYS AL-ASHʿARĪ [d. 42/622 or 52/672]. *Amīr*, or governor, of Basra and then of Kufa. He was named arbiter in the conflict that pitted ʿAlī against Muʿāwiya at Ṣiffīn. Also known for his successful military campaign Iraq. [Zabīdī 47; *EI*^{2} 1.716–17; cf. Ibn Ḥajar (1) 11.359–60]

ABŪ SAᶜĪD AḤMAD B. ᶜISĀ AL-KHARRĀZ [d. 277/890 or 286/899]. An important Sufi figure from Baghdad and close companion of other famous mystics—Dhū al-Nūn, Sarī al-Saqaṭī, Bishr al-Ḥāfī. Reputedly said that every exterior differs from the interior and is, therefore, false. He emphasized love. [Qushayrī 38; Sulamī 228–32]

ABŪ SULAYMĀN ᶜABD AL-RAHMĀN B. ᶜAṬIYYAH AL-DĀRĀNĪ [d. 205/820]. Though hailing from Wāsiṭ, Abū Sulaymān was an early influential exponent of Sufism in Syria. He later travelled to Dārayā (on the outskirts of Damascus), from which his name is derived. He is mentioned as having accepted *ḥadīths* from the celebrated traditionist and ascetic Sufyān al-Thawrī. Abū Sulaymān taught Ibn Abī al-Ḥawārī, with whom he consolidated Baṣran Sufism in Syria. In Baṣra, Mālik b. Dīnār had been the first to regularize Sufi teachings, but it was largely with ᶜUbayda ᶜAbd al-Wāḥid b. Zayd (d. 177/793), Abū Sulaymān al-Dārānī's teacher, that Sufism had taken root in that region. [Sulamī 76; Qushayrī 25; Ibn al-Mulaqqin 386–97; Jāmī 39–40, 65; Nabhānī II.144; Hujwīrī 143–44; Dhahabī I.203–07; Massignon, *Essai* 219]

ABŪ ᶜUBAYD MUḤAMMAD B. ḤASAN AL-BUSRĪ [d. 245/859]. One of the earliest mystics and sometimes compared to Dhū al-Nūn and Abū Turāb al-Nakhshī. Abū Saᶜīd al-Kharrāz and other famous Sufis knew him. He is reputed for his severe asceticism and poverty. [Qushayrī 37; Sulamī 147, 228]

ABŪ ᶜUTHMĀN AL-NĪSĀBŪRĪ [d. 298/910]. Hailed from Rayy, where he was a companion of Yaḥyā b. Muᶜādh al-Rāzī and Shah b. Shujāᶜ al-Kirmānī before travelling on to Nīsāpūr to accompany Abū Ḥifṣ. He taught, 'The heart is upright because of four traits: humility before God, poverty before God, fear of God and hope in God.' [Sulamī 170–75]

ABŪ YAᶜQŪB ISḤĀQ B. MUḤAMMAD AL-SŪSĪ AL-NAHRAJŪRĪ [d. 336/947]. Sage of Nahrajūrī, Abū Yaᶜqūb lived in Basra and Baghdad, where he was a companion of Junayd. [Jāmī I.129–30, no. 139]

ABŪ YAZĪD (BĀYAZĪD) ṬAYFŪR B. ᶜ ĪSĀ B. SURŪSHĀN AL-BISṬĀMĪ [261/874 or 264/877–8]—One of the most penetrating, influential mystics of Islam, Abū Yazīd nevertheless is reputed to have produced no writings. Instead, some five hundred of his sayings were preserved for posterity, thanks mainly to Abū Mūsā ᶜĪsā b. Ādam, his nephew. His sayings display such spiritual audacity that it is hardly surprising he should have occasionally run into trouble with certain authorities who were keen on imposing their interpretations of the faith or defining a particular form of orthodoxy, despite Sufism's undisputed role at every level of society—social, spiritual and intellectual. Abū Yazīd was said to have befriend Dhū al-Nūn al-Miṣrī. [*EI*^{2} online]

AḤMAD B. ḤANBAL [d. 241/855]. One of the best know traditionists, Ibn Ḥanbal is respected by most jurists and revered by Sufis. His critique of the speculative bent of the *mutakallimūn* helped alter the course of theological reasoning. After him, Islamic intellectual discourse was much more wary of the literal intentions of sacred writings and speech. He was a companion of Bishr al-Ḥāfī, and the Ḥanbalī legal school is named after him. [Abū Nuʿaym ix.161–234; *EI*^{2} i.272–7]

AḤMAD B. KHIḌRAWAYH AL-BALKHĪ [d. 240/854–55]. A prominent figure from Khurāsān and companion of Abū Ṭurāb al-Balkhī. Went to Nīshāpūr to visit Abū Ḥafs, then to Bisṭām to visit Abū Yazīd al-Bisṭāmī. Died when he was 95 years old. [Sulamī 93–7; Ṣafadī vi.373]

AL-AḤNAF B. QAYS AL-ʿANBAR AL-BAṢRĪ AL-TAMĪMĪ [d. 67/686–7]—A second-generation Muslim and the first from the Tamīm tribe to embrace Islam. He took an active part in important military campaigns in Iran. While he did not fight in the Battle of the Camel, he did join the Battle of Ṣiffīn. He was noted for his aphorisms and died in Kufa at seventy years old. [Ibn Khallikān i:635–44; *EI*^{2} i:304]

ʿALĪ B. ABĪ ṬĀLIB [d. 40/661]. A cousin and son-in-law of the Prophet. He accepted reluctantly to be the fourth caliph after ʿUthmān's assassination (and was later named *Imām* by Shīʿa Muslims). Sufis revere him for his breadth of knowledge, piety and ascetic mien. Died at Kufa by a poisoned arrow. [Ibn Ḥanbal, *K. al-zuhd* 47–52; Hujwīrī 101–02; *EI*^{2} ii.381–86]

ANAS B. MĀLIK [d. 91–3/709–11]. Anas was a young boy when the Prophet came to Medina. He transmitted a large number of traditions to his many students, who used them for their own collections. His transmissions are recorded by Bukhārī and Muslim. On the issue of written traditions, however, he insisted that '[we] do not value the knowledge of those who have not written down.' He took part in several military expeditions. [Nabhānī i.130; Ibn ʿAbd al-Barr, *Istīʿāb* no. 277; Azmi 49; *EI*^{2} i.482]

ʿAṬIYYA B. ʿABD AL-GHĀFIR. *See* ʿUqbah b. ʿAbd al-Ghāfir.

AYYŪB B. ABĪ TAYMIYYA SIKHTIYĀNĪ B. ABĪ TAMĪMA, ABŪ BAKR [d. 131/748–9]. He narrated traditions and was reputed for his strict devotion to the *Sunna*. His teacher was Anas b. Mālik. [Abū Nuʿaym iii.3–14; Azami 81]

BILĀL B. SAʿD B. TAMĪM AL-ASHʿARĪ [d. 120/738]. A traditionist and known for his eloquent preaching. Died under Caliph Hishām's reign. [Abū Nuʿaym v.221–34; Ibn al-Jawzī iv.190–93; Ibn Ḥajar, *Taqrīb* i.140, no. 782]

BISHR B. AL-ḤĀRITH AL-ḤĀFĪ [d. 226 or 227/841–42]. A companion of al-Fuḍayl b. ʿIyāḍ, Bishr 'the Barefooted' (because he considered even shoes 'a veil from God'). He hailed from Marw and lived in Baghdad. He was knowledgeable in the religious sciences, and taught that whoever wished to be honoured in this world and praised in the next must forgo three things: asking from others, vilifying others and accepting an invitation for a meal—since God alone, not the host, is the benefactor. [Abū Nuʿaym viii, 336; Sulamī 39–47; Ibn al-Jawzī ii.183–90; Ibn Khallikān i.274–77; Jāmī 48–9; Nabhānī i.607–08; Hujwīrī 135–6; Zabīdī 127; Schimmel 37–8; *EI*^{2} i.1282–84]

DĀ'ŪD B. AL-MUḤABBAR. Unidentified.

DĀ'ŪD B. NUṢAYR AL-ṬĀ'Ī, ABŪ SULAYMĀN [d. 160/776–77 or 162/778–79]. A Kufan contemporary of Ibrāhīm b. Adham and a pupil of Abū Ḥanīfa in jurisprudence and Ḥabīb Rāʿī in early 'Sufism'. However, he shunned the authority of certain professional scholars. Although learned from them, he preferred silence. He reputedly either buried his books or threw them into the Euphrates. His brand of asceticism was coloured by grief and seclusion. [Abū Nuʿaym vii.335–66; Hujwīrī 140–1; Ibn al-Jawzī iii.74–82; Ibn Khallikān ii.259–63; ʿAṭṭār 138–42; Nabhānī, *Karāmāt al-awliyā'* ii.63–4; Azmi 126]

DHŪ AL-NŪN AL-MIṢRĪ [d. 245/860]. Born at Ekhmim in Upper Egypt. He was renowned for his alchemist and mystical predilections, and was thought to understand Egyptian hieroglyphs. At one time, he was arrested on charges of heresy but was soon released. [Abū Nuʿaym ix.331–95; Sulamī 15–26; Ibn al-Jawzī iv.287–93; Ibn Khallikān i.315–18; Massignon, *Essai* 184–91; *EI*^{2} ii.249; cf. Ibn ʿArabī, *La vie merveilleuse*]

AL-FUḌAYL B. ʿIYAḌ [d. 187/803]. A native of Merv, Ibn ʿIyaḍ enjoyed a great reputation as mystic and is frequently cited in Sufi works. He steadfastly avoided the wealthy, abstaining from everything that he suspected might be tinged with worldliness. [Abū Nuʿaym viii.84–139; Sulamī 6–14; Ibn Jawzī ii.134–39; Ibn Khallikān iv.47–50; Jāmī 37–8; Nabhānī ii.440; *EI*^{2} ii.958]

AL-FUḌAYL B. ʿUBAYD. Unidentified.

AL-ḤAKĪM. Unidentified.

ḤAMMĀD B. ABĪ SULAYMĀN. Unidentified.

AL-ḤĀRITH B. ASAD AL-MUḤĀSIBĪ [d. 243/857]. A Shāfiʿī jurist—like Ghazālī, who was influenced by his thought—and a *mutakallim*. Despite his refutation of the Muʿtazilites, he was still accused by Aḥmad b. Ḥanbal of failing to eradicate the speculative elements of *kalām*. [Qushayrī 20; Watt 282]

AL-ḤASAN B. ʿALĪ [d. 49/669]. Grandson of the Prophet and second *Imām* in Shīʿa tradition. He lived a secluded life in Medina while his father was alive, before laying claim to the caliphate. [*EI*² 290f] [*EI*² III.240–43; Bauer 29]

AL-ḤASAN AL-BAṢRĪ [d. 110/728]. One of the most outstanding intellectual figures in early *kalām*, al-Ḥasan participated in the major political and philosophical debates of his time. He was considered a distant forerunner of Muʿtazilism, on certain doctrinal emphases, but was especially respected for the ascetic life he led. [Abū Nuʿaym II.131–61; Ibn Khallikān II.69–73; Dhahabī (2) i.71–2, no. 66; Nabhānī II.21; Hujwīrī 115–16; Massignon, *Essai* 174–201; Watt 64, 103–4ff; *EI*² III.254–55]

ʿIBĀDA B. ṢĀMIT [d. 34–5/654–55]. Died in Ramala.

IBN ʿABBĀS, ʿABD ALLĀH [68/687–78]. A cousin and companion of the Prophet Muḥammad, Ibn ʿAbbās was highly respected for his piety and knowledgeable commentaries on the Qur'an, the exegesis of which he is generally thought to have legitimised. He fought ʿAlī at the Battle of Ṣiffīn. [Abū Nuʿaym I.314–29; *EI*² I.40–1]

IBN MASʿŪD [d. 32/652–3]—One of the earliest converts, a famous Companion of the Prophet and a reader of the Qur'ān. At first, he possessed little political power, contenting himself with rendering personal service to the Prophet, who employed him. Thanks to this close association, Ibn Masʿūd—of Bedouin origin—received the Qur'ān directly from the Prophet's lips. Later, he became an authoritative source for information about the Prophet's *miʿrāj* (nocturnal journey) and the Night of Power. He is also thought to have been the first to read the Qur'ān in public. During the Meccan persecution, he travelled to Abyssinia with Miqdād b. ʿAmr. He was at the Battles of Badr and Uḥud, where in particular he denounced some fighters' penchant for greed and plunder. He participated in the campaign against a pagan rebellion encamped around Medina. Honest, he was entrusted with booty during the battle of the Yarmūk, under the reign of Abū Bakr. After the Prophet's passing, he became administrator, ambassador and caller to the faith. Although considered politically shrewd by then, he was highly admired for his personal integrity and learnedness, which led him into a relatively sophisticated interpretation of the Qur'ān. [*EI*² online]

IBN AL-MUSAYYIB, ABŪ MUḤAMMAD SAʿD [d. 93/711]. One of the most learned scholars of the second generation. A pious figure, Ibn al-Musayyib used to give himself the appearance of a religious 'hypocrite', to deepen his piety—a practice approved and even praised by many Sufis. [Abū Nuʿaym II.161–76; al-Nabhānī I.149; Hujwīrī 116]

IBRĀHĪM B. ADHAM B. MANṢŪR [d. 161/778–8)—Born in Balkh, Khurāsān, where his father was governor, Ibrāhīm was one of the most important Sufis in his time, celebrated for his asceticism and generosity. After abandoning worldliness, he travelled to Mecca, where he accompanied Sufyān al-Thawrī and al-Fuḍayl b. ʿIyāḍ. He disapproved of begging and worked hard with his own hands. His unusual focus and deep devotion led him to join two expeditions against the Byzantine rulers, where he finally died. [Abū Nuʿaym v:318; Sulamī 27–38; Jāmī 41–3; Zabīdī 283; *EI*^{2} online]

IBRĀHĪM B. AḤMAD AL-KHAWWĀṢ, ABŪ ISḤĀQ [d. 291/903–4]. Associated with Junayd's circle. Famed for his piety and spiritual discipline, he used to wander the deserts without provisions, relying solely on the *ʿaṭā' al-tawakkul*—namely, the gift of reliance granted by God. [Abū Nuʿaym x.325–31; Ibn Jawzī iv.80–4; Jāmī 136–9; Zabīdī 285, 372; Schimmel 119]

ʿĪSĀ B. KATHĪR [AL-ASADĪ]. Unidentified.

JĀBIR B. ʿABD ALLĀH AL-SALAMĪ AL-ANṢARĪ [d. 78/697]. Eminent Companion of the Prophet and transmitter of numerous *ḥadīths*. His role is particularly appreciated in Shīʿa tradition. Died in Medina after numerous military exploits on the frontiers of Islam. [Dhahabī (2) i.43–4, no. 21; Ibn al-Mubārak 1102; *EI*^{2}, Sup. 230–32]

JAʿFAR AL-ṢĀDIQ, ABŪ ʿABD ALLĀH [148/765]. Sixth *Imām* in Shīʿa tradition and highly venerated by Sufis. Known especially as a traditionist and author of a mystical commentary on the Qur'an. He was also the source of inspiration of Jābir b. Ḥayyān, the famous alchemist. Died in Medina. [Abū Nuʿaym iii.192–206; Ibn Jawzī ii.94–8; Ibn Khallikān i.327–28]

JUNAYD, ABŪ AL-QĀSIM B. MUḤAMMAD [d. 298/910–11]. One of the most influential figures in early Sufism who traced his roots to Nāhavand, the ancient royal capital of the Sassanians. He learned from Sarī al-Saqaṭī and al-Hārith al-Muḥāsibī. [Abū Nuʿaym x.255–87; Sulamī 155–63; Ibn Khallikān i.373–75 *EI*^{2} ii.384–85]

MANṢŪR AL-DĪNAWARĪ. Unidentified.

MAʿRŪF AL-KARKHĪ [d. 200/815–16]. An important early Sufi figure, and one of the most revered, Maʿrūf was particularly known for his great piety and *futuwwa*. He taught Sarī al-Saqaṭī and was a companion of Dā'ūd al-Ṭā'ī. [Qushayrī 15–6; Sulamī 83–90]

MAYMŪN B. MAHRĀN. Unidentified.

MUʿĀDH B. JABAL AL-KHAZRAJ [d. 14/635]. The Prophet's governor in Yemen, Muʿādh was an early convert to Islam whose legal opinion was respected. [Winter 301]

MUʿĀWIYA B. ABĪ SUFYĀN B. ḤARB B. UMAYYA [r. 40–60/661–80]. The first member of the Umayya tribe to become caliph. His conflict with ʿAlī and his supporters was severe enough to cause a major rift among Muslims over the succession to the caliphate.

MUʿĀWIYA B. QURRA. Unidentified.

MUḤAMMAD B. ʿALĪ B. JAʿFAR AL-KATTĀNĪ, ABŪ BAKR [d. 322/933–4]. Hailed from Baghdad—where he was a member of the Sufi circles of Junayd, Kharrāz and Nūrī—and travelled to Mecca, where he died. He used to preach, 'Be in this world with your body, but in the next be with your heart.' [Abū Nuʿaym x.357–58; Qushayrī 45; Sulamī 373–77]

MUḤAMMAD B. SAʿĪD [B. IBRĀHĪM]. Unidentified.

MUḤAMMAD B. SAʿĪD AL-MARWAZĪ. Unidentified.

MUJĀHID B. JABR [d. 103/721–22]. Respected traditionist from Mecca, despite his Kharājite sympathies. Also known for his Qur'anic exegesis. [Abū Nuʿaym III.279–310; Ibn Jawzī II.117–19; Dhahabī (2) I.92–3, no. 83; *EI²* VII.295]

MUSʿAB B. SAʿD AL-MADANĪ [d. 103/720–21]. Respected traditionist from Medina who reported the sayings of ʿAlī b. Abī Ṭālib. [Dhahabī, *al-ʿIbār* I.95]

MUṬARRIF B. ʿABD ALLĀH B. AL- SHIKHKHĪR AL-TĀBIʿĪ AL-BAṢRĪ [d. 95/713–14]. Holy man and popular storyteller in Basra. [Abū Nuʿaym II.198–212; Ibn Jawzī II.144–49; Ibn Khallikān v.211; Dhahabī (2) I, 64–5, no. 54]

AL-RAMLĪ, MUḤAMMAD B. AḤMAD ABŪ BAKR IBN AL-NĀBULUSĪ [d. 363/973]—A traditionist who hailed from Nābulus and became *ra'īs* of Ramla. He was influential among those learned in Damascus and Baghdad who considered themselves *Ahl al-Ḥadīth*, in opposition to the Ashʿarīs. He was known for his retreats with disciples in the Akuwākh Bāniyās ('the huts of Bāniyās'), at the foot of Mt. Hermon in the Syrian Jawlān. He was finally executed by Caliph al-Muʿizz for his strident public opposition to Fāṭimid rule over Syria. [*EI²* online]

RUWAYM B. AḤMAD AL-BAGHDĀDĪ, ABŪ MUḤAMMAD [d. 303/915–16]. A mystic from Baghdad, Ruwaym combined, according to the Ẓāhirite school of *fiqh*, Sufism with *fiqh*. He studied and taught the Qur'an. [Abū Nuʿaym x.296–302; Sulamī 180–84; Ibn Jawzī II.249–50; Ibn al-Mulaqqin 228–31; Jāmī I.94–7]

SAʿD B. MUʿĀDH [lived during the Prophet's time]—He is described as the strongest of the al-Aws tribesmen whose influence drew many people into the fold of Islam, gaining the early community crucial support and alliances. Opposed to Islam at first, Saʿd later became its most influential supporter in Medina, especially at the critical time of the *Hijra*. He was the most prominent of the Anṣār at the battle of Badr, where he accompanied the Prophet Muḥammad and arranged for his safety. His chief talent appears to lie in dealing with the intense political intrigue at the time. During the pagan Meccans's siege of Medina, at the battle of the Khandaq, he managed to blunt the menacing impact of betrayal by the Jewish Qurayẓa clan, who negotiated secretly with the enemy and with whom elements of al-Aws were allied. [*EI*[2] online]

SAʿD B. MUʿĀDH [B. AL-NUʿMĀN]. Unidentified.

SAHL B. ʿABD ALLĀH AL-TUSTARĪ, ABŪ MUḤAMMAD [d. 282/896]. Studied with Sufyān al-Thawrī and said to have met Dhū al-Nūn in Mecca on his pilgrimage. A commentary on the Qur'an is attributed to him. His contributions to Sufism were both practical and theoretical—the latter includes his theory of revealed light. He had a reputation for strict spiritual exercises. [Abū Nuʿaym i.189; Sulamī 206–11; Jāmī i.66–8; Nabhānī ii.110]

SĀLIM B. ʿABD ALLĀH [d. 106/724]. Sālim was one of the seven leading *fuqahā'* at the time. His authority was recognized by many, and he was compared to his father for his good judgement and religious steadfastness. [Zabīdī ii]

SARĪ AL-SAQAṬĪ, ABŪ ḤASAN B. AL-MUGHALLIS [d. 251/865 or 253/867]. The maternal uncle and teacher of Junayd, Sarī was the acknowledged leader of Baghdad's Sufi circles. His own teacher was Maʿrūf Karkhī. He classified the spiritual 'states' (*aḥwāl*) and decanted on the unicity (*tawḥīd*) of God. His musings, however, earned him the criticism of Ibn Ḥanbal, especially on sensitive issues relating to theology. [Abū Nuʿaym x.116–27; Ibn Jawzī ii.209–18; Sulamī 48–55; Ibn Khallikān ii.357–59; Jāmī i.53–4; Hujwīrī 141–2; Ibn al-Mulaqqin 160–65]

SUFYĀN AL-THAWRĪ [d. *ca.* 161/777]. A celebrated traditionist, ascetic and jurist, al-Thawrī was extraordinarily knowledgeable in the scriptural sources of Islam, and sometimes rated even higher than Mālik b. Anas. He was one of the first to commit prophetic traditions to writing. He was also actively engaged in many theological debates and founded a *madhhab*, or legal school, that is now extinct. Often harassed by powerful figures, he was forced to flee several times. [Abū Nuʿaym vi.356–vii.143; Dhahabī (2) i.203–7, no. 198; Ibn Jawzī iii.82–7; Ibn Khallikān ii.386–91; Nabhānī 98; *EI*[1] vii.500–2]

ṬĀ'ŪS B. KAYSĀN AL-YAMĀNĪ [d. 106/725]. Belonged to the 'succeeding generation', or *tābiʿūn*. [Zabīdī 31; cf. Ibn Mubārak 1118, no. 240]

ʿUMAR B. ʿABD AL-ʿAZĪZ [d. 110/728; *r.* 99–101/717–20]. ʿUmar II became caliph in 99/717. Although his reign lasted less than two-and-a-half years, he left a deep impact on the people he ruled. He is considered far more pious and just than most of his Umayyad predecessors. His aggressive, though relatively non-sectarian, policies won him broad support from Muslims, including hitherto marginalized sects. [Masʿūdī III.192–205; Dhahabī (2) I.118–21, no. 104; Abū Nuʿaym V.253–353; Ṣafadī III.133; Hodgson I.268]

ʿUMAR B. AL-KHAṬṬĀB [d. 23/644; *r.* 13/634 to 23/644]. His conversion, at 26 years old, altered the circumstances of Muslims, who had led a clandestine existence until then during the Prophet's lifetime. He also played a key role in the election of Abū Bakr as the first caliph of Islam. Under his reign, the realm of Islam expanded to Syria, Mesopotamia, Armenia, Iran, Egypt and North Africa—until he was assassinated. [Abū Nuʿaym I.38–55; Ibn Jawzī I.101–12; Ibn Ḥajar (2) II.518–19, no. 5736]

ʿUQBA B. ʿABD AL-GHĀFIR [d. 183/799]. A transmitter of traditions. [Cf. Zabīdī 81]

WAHB B. MUNABBIH AL-YAMĀNĪ [d. 114/732–33]. A traditionist from Sanʿā who compiled many books on the lives of past prophets (a genre known as *isrā'iliyyāt*), some portions of which have been preserved in Ṭabarānī's *al-Muʿjam al-kabīr*. [Abū Nuʿaym IV.23–82; Ibn Jawzī II.164–67; Ibn Khallikān VI.35–6; Dhahabī (2) I.100–1, no. 93; Azmi 104–5]

YAḤYĀ B. MUʿĀDH AL-RĀZĪ [d. 258/871–72]. Lived in Balkh and Nīshāpūr, where he died. He was a disciple of Ibn Karrām. One of the greatest preachers in his time and the first to teach about Sufism in public, Yaḥyā was frequently cited in spiritual works. He emphasized hope in God. [Sulamī 107–14; Abū Nuʿaym X.51–70; Ibn Jawzī IV.71–80; Ibn Khallikān VI.165–68; Massignon, *Essai* 268–72]

YAʿQŪB AL-MAKFŪF. Unidentified.

YAZĪD B. AL-ḤĀRITH. Unidentified.

BIBLIOGRAPHY

The Book of Intention, Sincerity and Truthfulness

A = Ghazālī, Abū Ḥāmid Muḥammad. *Iḥyāʾ ʿulūm al-dīn*. Vol. 14. Cairo: Lajnat Nashr al-Thaqāfa al-Islāmiyya, 1357 AH. With marginal notes by Zayn al-Dīn al-ʿIrāqī.

B = Al-Zabīdī, Muḥammad b. Muḥammad al-Ḥusayn. *Itḥāf al-sāda al-muttaqīn bi-sharḥ Iḥyāʾ ʿulūm al-dīn*. Vol. 10. Cairo: Dar al-Fikr, n.d.

Bauer, Hans. *Über Intention, reine Absicht und Wahrhaftigkeit. Das 37. Buch von al-Gazâlî's Hauptwerk*. Translation of 'Intention, Sincerity and Truthfulness' with notes. Halle: Verlag Von Max Niemeyer, 1916.

Other Sources

Abū Nuʿaym Aḥmad b. ʿAbd Allāh al-Isbahānī. *Ḥilyat al-awliyāʾ wa-ṭabaqāt al-aṣfiyāʾ*. Cairo: Maṭbaʿat al-Saʿāda, 1933/1351.

ʿAṭṭār, Farīd al-Dīn. *Muslim Saints and Mystics*. Translated by A. J. Arberry. London: Routledge & Kegan Paul, 1966.

Azmi, Mohammad Mustafa. *Studies in Early Ḥadīth Literature*. Indianapolis: American Trust Publications, 1978.

al-Bayḍāwī, Naṣīr al-Dīn. *Anwār al-tanzīl wa-asrār al-taʾwīl*. Lithographed. N.p.: Dār al-Jīl, 1329 AH.

Al-Bukhārī, Abū ʿAbd Allāh Muḥammad b. Ismāʿīl. *Saḥīḥ*. Beirut: Al-Maktaba al-Thaqāfiyya, n.d.

Al-Dhahabī (1), Shams al-Dīn. *Al-ʿIbar fī khabar man ghabar*. Ed. Basyūnī Zaghlūl. 4 vols. Beirut 1985.

Al-Dhahabī (2), Abū ʿAbd Allāh Shams al-Dīn. *Tadhkīrāt al-ḥuffāẓ*. 4 vols. Hyderabad-Daccan: Majlis Dāʾirat al-Maʿārif al-ʿUthmāniyya, 1968/1388.

Dozy, R.P.A. *Dictionnaire détaillé des noms des vêtements chez les arabes*. Amsterdam, 1845.

Encyclopaedia of Islam. Ed. M. Houtsama *et al.* Leiden, 1927. Second edition, ed J. H. Kramers, *et al.* Leiden, 1954-.

Encyclopaedia of Islam, second edition. Edited by P. Bearman, Th. Bianquis, C.E. Bosworth, E. van Donzel, W.P. Heinrichs. Brill Online, 2013. Reference: McGill University. 6 December 2013.

Ghazālī, Abū Ḥāmid Muḥammad. *Al-Munqidh min al-ḍalāl* [Arabic and French texts]. 2nd edition. Introduced, annotated and translated by Farid Jabre. Beirut: Commission libanaise pour la traduction des chefs-d'œvres, 1969.

———. *Mizān al-ʿamal*. Cairo; Maṭbaʿat Kurdistān al-ʿIlmiyya, 1328/1910.

———. *Al-Maqṣad al-asnā fī sharḥ maʿānī asmāʾ Allāh al-ḥusnā*. Beirut, 1971.

———. *Minhāj al-ʿābidīn*. Beirut: Mu'assasat al-Risāla, 1989/1409.

Gimaret, Daniel. *Théorie de l'acte humain en théologie musulmane*. Paris: Librairie Philosophique J. Vrin, 1980.

Al-Ḥakīm, Suʿād. *Muʿjam al-ṣūfiyya: al-Ḥikma fī ḥudūd al-kalima*. Beirut: D. Nadrah, 1981/1401.

Hujwīrī. *Kashf al-maḥjūb li-arbāb al-qulūb*. [French translation: Djamshid Mortazavi. *Somme spirituelle*. Paris: Sindbad, 1988.]

Ibn ʿAbd al-Barr, Yūsuf b. ʿAbd Allāh. *Al-Istīʿāb fī maʿrifat al-aṣḥāb*. Cairo: Ed. M. al-Bijāwī, n.d.

Ibn ʿArabī, Muḥyī al-Dīn. Ibn ʿArabī, Muhyiddin. *Fuṣūṣ al-ḥikam*. Beirut: Dār al-Kitāb al-ʿArabī, 1980 CE/1400 AH.

———. *Al-Futūḥāt al-makkiyya*. Cairo: Al-Hay'a al-Miṣriyya al-ʿĀmma lil-Kitāb, 1985/1405-1992/1412.

———. *Al-Kawkab al-durrī fī manāqib Dhī al-Nūn al-Miṣrī*. [French translation: Roger Deladrière. *La vie merveilleuse de Dhû-l-Nûn l'Egyptien*. Paris: Sindbad, 1988.

Ibn Bābawayh, Abū Jaʿfar Muḥammad b, ʿAlī b. al-Ḥusayn b. *Kitāb al-khisāl*. Edited and annotated by ʿAlī Akbar al-Ghaffārī. Tehrān: Maktabat al-Ṣaddūq, n.d.

Ibn Ḥajar (1) al-ʿAsqalānī, Shihāb al-Dīn. *Al-Isāba fī tamyīz al-ṣaḥāba*. 4 vols. Beirut, n.d.

———. *Taqrīb al-tahdhīb*. 2 vols. Ed. ʿAbd al-Qādir ʿAṭā'. Beirut, 1993.

Ibn Ḥanbal, Aḥmad. *Kitāb al-zuhd*. Beirut: Dār al-Nahḍa al-ʿArabiyya, 1981.

Ibn Jawzī, Abū al-Faraj. *Ṣifāt al-ṣafwā*. 4 vols. Hyderabad, 1936.

Ibn Khallikān, Abū al-ʿAbbās. *Wafayāt al-aʿyān*. 8 vols. Ed. Iḥsān ʿAbbās. Beirut, n.d.

Ibn Maja, al-Qazwīnī, Abū ʿAbd Allāh Muḥammad b. Yazīd. *Sunan*. Cairo: Dār Iḥyā' al-Kutub al-ʿArabiyya, 1918/1326.

Ibn al-Mubārak, ʿAbd Allāh. *Al-Zuhd wal-raqā'iq*. N.p.: Dār al-Miʿrāj al-Dawliyya lil-Nashr, 1995.

Ibn al-Mulaqqin, ʿUmar ʿAlī. *Ṭabaqāt al-awliyā'*. Beirut: Dār al-Maʿārif, 1986/1406.

Ibn Rushd, Abū Walīd Muḥammad b. Aḥmad. *Bidāyat al-mujtahid.* N.p.: Dār al-Fikr, n.d.

Ibn Saʿd, Muḥammad b. Saʿd b. Māniʿ al-Zuhrī. *Kitāb al-tabaqāt al-kabīr.* I-X. Ed. Eduard Sachau. Leiden: E. J. Brill, 1917.

Jāmī, ʿAbd al-Raḥmān b. Aḥmad. *Nafaḥāt al-uns min ḥaḍarāt al-quds.* N.p.: Kitābfurūsh Saʿdī, 1337 AH.

Jurjānī, al-Sayyid al-Sharīf. *Kitāb al-taʿrīfāt.* Beirut: Dār al-Kutub al-ʿIlmiyya, 1983.

Kalābādhī, Abū Bakr Muḥammad b. Isḥāq. *Al-Taʿarruf li-madhhab ahl al-taṣawwuf.* Beirut: Dār al-Kutub al-ʿIlmiyya, 1993. [Translated as *The Doctrine of the Sufis* by A. J. Arberry. Cambridge: Cambridge University Press, 1991.]

Al-Kharrāz, Abū Saʿīd Aḥmad b. ʿĪsā. *The Book of Truthfulness* (*Kitab Al-Ṣidq*). Edited and translated by Arthur John Arberry. London: Published for the Islamic Research Association by Humphrey Milford Oxford University Press, 1937.

Khaṭīb al-Baghdādī. *Tarīkh Baghdād.* Cairo, 1349.

Lisān al-ʿArab. By Ibn Manẓūr al-Ifrīqī, Abū al-Faḍl Jamāl al-Dīn Muḥammad

Makkī, Abū Ṭālib. *Qūt al-qulūb.* Cairo: Al-Mabaʿa al-Maymaniyya, 1310 AH.

Massignon, Louis. *Essai sur les origines du lexique technique de la mystique musulmane.* Paris: Librairie philosophique J. Vrin, 1954.

Muslim, Abū al-Ḥusayn Muslim b. al-Ḥajjāj. *Ṣaḥīḥ.* Cairo: Dār al-Ḥadīth, 1418/1997.

Masʿūdī, Abū al-Ḥasan. *Murūj al-dhahab.* 4 vols. Ed. ʿAbd al-Ḥamīd. Beirut:, n.d.

Al-Nabhānī, Yūsuf b. Ismāʿīl. *Jāmiʿ karāmāt al-awliyā'.* Cairo: Dār al-Kutub al-ʿArabīya al-Kubrā, 1329 AH.

Al-Qāshānī, Kamāl al-Dīn ʿAbd al-Razzāq. *Iṣṭilāḥāt al-ṣūfiya.* Second edition. Introduced and annotated by Dr. Muḥammad Kamāl Ibrāhīm Jaʿfar. Qom: Intishārāt Bīdār, 1370 AHS.

Qushayrī, Abū al-Qāsim. *Risāla.* Cairo: Maṭbaʿat Muḥammad ʿAlī Sabīh, 1966/1386.

Ṣafadī, Ṣalāḥ al-Dīn Khalīl b. Aybak. *Al-Wāfī bil-wafiyāt.* Ed. H. Ritter *et al.* Jamʿiyyat al-Mustashriqīn al-Almāniyya, 1962.

Schimmel, Annemarie. *Mystical Dimensions of Islam.* Chapel Hill: The University of North Carolina Press, 1975.

Shaker, Anthony F. *Thinking in the Language of Reality: Ṣadr al-Dīn Qūnavī (d. 1274 CE) and the Mystical Philosophy of Reason.* Xlibris, 2012.

Shaʿrānī, ʿAbd al-Wahhāb. *Al-Ṭabaqāt al-kubrā.* 2 vols. Cairo, 1317.

Sulamī, Abū ʿAbd al-Raḥmān. *Ṭabaqāt al-ṣūfiyya.* Cairo: Maktabat al-Khānjā, 1987/1406.

Ṭabarī, Abū Jaᶜfar Muḥammad b. Jarīr. *Ta'rīkh Ṭabarī*. Cairo: Dār al-Turāth, 1969.

Tirmidhī, Abū ᶜĪsā Muḥammad. *Al-Jāmiᶜ al-Ṣaḥīḥ*. N.p.: Dār al-Fikr, 1978/1398.

Wensinck, A.J. *Concordance et indices de la tradition musulmane*. Leiden, 1936.

Winter, T. J. *The Remembrance of Death and the Afterlife*. Cambridge: The Islamic Texts Society, 1995.

Watt, Montgomery. *The Formative Period of Islamic Thought*. Oxford, UK: Oneworld Publications, 1973, re-edited 1998.

Al-Zabīdī, Muḥammad b. Muḥammad al-Ḥusayn. *Itḥāf al-sāda al-muttaqīn bi-sharḥ Iḥyā' ᶜulūm al-dīn*. Vol. 10. Cairo: Dar al-Fikr, n.d.

INDEX TO QUR'ĀNIC QUOTATIONS

SŪRA	VERSE	PAGE
I. *al-Fātiḥa*	5	87
II. *al-Baqara*	50	82
	177	94
	256	xxxvi–xxxvii
III. *Āl ʿImrān*	200	29
IV. *al-Nisā'*	35	5
	40	73
	146	49
VI. *al-Anʿām*	52	5, 42
	79	87
	108	32
IX. *al-Tawba*	75	91
	75–7	91
XI. *Hūd*	15	50n
	118	43
	119	43
XV. *al-Ḥijr*	40	52
XVI. *al-Naḥl*	66	53n, 57
XVII. *al-Isrā'*	44	xx
XVIII. *al-Kahf*	103–104	61
	110	49, 75, 76
XIX. *Maryam*	30	87
	41	81
	54	81
	56	81
	93	xxix
XX. *Ṭā Hā*	78	97
XXI. *al-Anbiyā'*	7	25
XXII. *al-Ḥajj*	37	20, 22
XXV. *al-Furqān*	25	2
XXX. *al-Rūm*	32	43

SŪRA	VERSE	PAGE
XXXI. *Luqmān*	22	xxxvi–xxxvii
XXXIII. *al-Aḥzāb*	8	84
	23	81, 90, 91
XXXVIII. *Ṣād*	83	63
XXXIX. *al-Zumar*	3	49
	47–9	61
	60	82
XLIV. *al-Dukhkhān*	54	42n
XLVII. *Muḥammad*	31	9
XLIX. *al-Ḥujurāt*	15	94, 97
L. *Qāf*	18	34
LII. *al-Ṭūr*	20	42n
LV. *al-Raḥmān*	72	42n
LVI. *al-Wāqiʿa*	22	42n
LVII. *al-Ḥadīd*	1	xix
LXIII. *al-Munāfiqūn*	1	88
XCVIII. *al-Bayyina*	4	1
	5	49
XCIX.w *al-Zalzala*	7–8	72–3

INDEX

ʿAbd al-ʿAzīz b. Abī Dā'ūd, 77
ʿAbd al-Wāḥid b. Zayd al-Baṣrī, 94
ablution, xxxi, 59
Abraham, 15n, 81
abstaining (*kaff*), 29
Abū Bakr al-Ṣiddīq, 62, 89–90, 92
Abū Bakr al-Warrāq, 97
Abū Bakr al-Warrāq al-Tirmidhī, 83
Abū Bakra, 8
Abū al-Dardā', 44
Abū Dharr, 94
Abū Hurayra, 8, 9, 50, 75
Abū Mūsā al-Ashʿarī, 52, 75
act/action, 1; avoiding action for fear of fault, 77–8; *bāṭin*/*ẓāhir* dynamics, xxxvi, 77n, 92–4; categories, 24; heart/limbs relationship, 20–1; human act, xxiii, xxv, xviiin (elements of, xxxiv–xxxv); human agency, xxv–xxvi, xxviiin; legally permitted act/*mubāḥ*, 43; meritorious act, 35, 43n; ostentation, 78; permitted acts/*mubāḥāt*, 24, 31–4 (intention, 28, 33); power, xxxv, 11, 12–13; refraining from acting, 35; sincerity, 55, 56; sinful acts/*maʿāṣī*, 24–8; truthfulness in action, xxxvii, 83, 85, 92–4; virtuous act, 43; will, xxxv, 11; see also good deed; intention/action relationship; pious deeds
Adam, 15n
Afterlife, see Hereafter
al-Aḥnaf b. Qays, 8
ʿAlī b. Abī Ṭālib, 44, 49
almsgiving, xxxi, 59; ostentation, 15, 50, 53, 58, 74–7; resolution, 89, 91
Anas b. Mālik, 6, 39n, 90
Anas b. al-Naḍr, 90
angel, 34, 50, 57n, 64n, 66; Gabriel, 15n, 95–6; Isrāfīl, 95–6; recording of intention, 5, 7, 55; truthfulness, 92, 94, 96
Antichrist (*Dajjāl*), 25
Aquinas, Thomas, St, xxiii
Arabic language, xxii, 54n
ʿArafa, Day of, 14–15, 54
Arberry, Arthur John, 92n
association (*shirk*), 59, 75, 76; association and sincerity, 57, 67, 76, 78; heart, 57; *shirk* contradicts *tawḥīd*, 57n; see also idolatry; sincerity
Ayyūb al-Sikhtiyānī, 53

bāʿith, see motive
balance (*mizān*), xxv, xxvii
al-Balkhī, Aḥmad b. Khiḍrawayh, 43
al-Baqillānī, Abū Bakr, 65
baṣīr, see insight
Battle of Badr, 90
Battle of Uḥud, 90–1
al-Bayḍāwī, Nāṣir al-Dīn, xxxiii, 42n

beauty of character (*ḥusn al-khuluq*), 81
Bilāl b. Saᶜd, 9–10
Bint al-Naḍr, 90
Bishr b. al-Ḥārith al-Ḥāfī, 81
al-Bisṭāmī, Abū Yazīd, 43
al-Busrī, Abū ᶜUbayd Muḥammad b. Ḥasan, 54

calumny, 32
child, xxviii, 33, 38
Companions of the Prophet, 49, 96, 97
contemplation (*fikr*), 19, 20
contentment, 56
Corbin, Henry, xxxiii
creation, xxix–xxx

Dajjāl, see Antichrist
al-Dārānī, Abū Sulaymān, 52, 82
Dā'ūd b. al-Muḥabbar, 39
Dā'ūd al-Ṭā'ī, 8
David, 82
Day of Questioning and Account, 34–5
debt, 8
desire, 12, 24, 38, 40, 60, 82, 83, 86, 88, 94
deviation (*ilḥād*), 58, 82
devil, 71, 77; battling the, 44; delivering from devil through sincerity, 52; devil's deception, 25, 26, 62, 68–71; knowledge, 27; prayer, 68, 70; sincerity, 61–3, 64n, 66, 68, 70; see also Iblīs
devoutness (*taqwā*), 20, 22, 97
dhawq, see experience
Dhū al-Nūn al-Miṣrī, 83
dīn, see religion
al-Dīnawarī, Manṣūr 81–2
discernment, 32, 77, 83
disciple, 9, 44–5, 68; see also learning; teaching
disobedience, 2, 76; see also obedience
dissimulation (*riyā'*), 28n; pious act, 28
duty, 30n, 35, 40, 51
eating, 35–6, 37, 40, 41, 44, 60; food, xxviii, 11–12, 33; properly gained nourishment, 82, 83
Eve, 15n
existence, xxix–xxx
experience (*dhawq*), xxv, xxvi, xxviii

faith, xxxi, xxxv, 38, 94, 94
falsafa, xxiin, xxiv, xxx; *falāsifa*, xxi–xxii, xxvii, xxix; *Tahāfut al-falāsifa*, xxiv; see also philosophy
family, xxviii, 33
al-Fārābī, Abū Naṣr, xiin
fasting, xxvii, 29; Day of ᶜArafa, 14–15; intention, xxvii, xxxi; sincerity, 58, 59
fear: avoiding action for fear of fault, 77–8; fear as motivation, 41, 65; fear of God, 83, 96; station of fear, 92n, 94, 95, 96
fighter, 30, 44, 89; intention, 6, 7, 22, 50; sincerity, 55, 74, 75, 76
fikr, see contemplation
food, see eating
forefathers (*al-salaf*), xxxvi, 8, 9, 27–8, 34, 38–9, 40
forgiveness, 44
al-Fuḍayl b. ᶜIyaḍ, 9, 66, 78
al-Fuḍayl b. ᶜUbayd, 91
funeral, 39, 59, 97

generosity (*sakhā'*), 26–7, 83; sincerity, 50
al-Ghazālī, Abū Ḥāmid, xix, 54n; human agency, xxv–xxvi, xxviiin; *Mizān al-ʿamal*, xxiii; *al-Munqidh min al-ḍalāl*, xxiv, xxv; philosopher and theologian, xxiii–xxiv, xxix; *Tahāfut al-falāsifa*, xxiv; see also *Iḥyā' ʿulūm al-dīn*
God, xxi; attributes, 26–7; beauty, 41, 42–3; the Creator, xxix–xxx, xxxiii; Divine Names (*al-Ḥayy*, xxxv; *al-Muḥyī*, xxxv; *Rabb al-ʿālamīn*, xxxiii); God's succour, xxxiv, 8; knowledge of God, 18–19; majesty, 41, 43, 70; meeting with God, 18; relationship with, xxvi, xxix–xxx
godfearing, xxviii, 8, 29
good deed, 5, 18, 22, 30, 33–5, 41, 56, 61, 91; Day of Resurrection, 33–4, 53; dissimulation, 28n; distinction from offence through sincerity, 53; intention, 40 (categories, 41); ostentation, 74–5; see also act/action; pious deeds
gratitude (*shukr*), 81
guidance (*hidāya*), 11, 30, 70

al-Ḥakīm, 82
al-Ḥakīm, Suʿād, xxx
Ḥammād b. Abī Sulaymān, 39
al-Ḥasan b. ʿAlī, 30
al-Ḥasan al-Baṣrī, xxxii, 9, 34, 39, 49, 94
ḥayā', see modesty
heart, 11, 20; association, 57; cheating of the heart, 71; devoutness, 22; effect of pious acts on, 21, 22; heart/limbs relationship, 20–1; Hereafter, 61; inclination of, 24–5; intention, xxxiii, 32–3, 40 (heart as loci of intention, 5); lying, 88–9; sincerity, 49, 57, 59, 61, 71; superioriority of the act of the heart, 20
Hell: fear of, 65; Fire, 81, 95; intention, xxxii, 8, 9, 33, 34, 40, 41; sincerity, lack of, 50
Hereafter, 27, 29, 41n; heart, 61; intention, xxxiv, 7, 32, 41, 52; pious deeds, 18, 19, 20; Qur'ān, 41n; sincerity, 60, 61, 77n
hidāya, see guidance
houris (*ḥūr al-ʿayn*) 42n
humility, 21, 69, 83, 93
ḥusn al-khuluq, see beauty of character
hypocrisy, xxxvi, 1–2, 28n, 36, 69, 88–9, 91

ʿibāda, see worship
ʿIbāda b. Ṣāmit, 6, 75
Iblīs (Satan), 50–2; see also devil
Ibn ʿAbbās, 81, 83
Ibn Abī al Waqqāṣ, 49
Ibn ʿArabī, Muḥyi al-Dīn Muḥammad, xxiv, xxix, xxx–xxxi, 54n
Ibn Ḥanbal, Aḥmad, xix, 27–8, 39
Ibn Kaʿb, 6n
Ibn Masʿūd, 6, 75
Ibn al-Musayyib, Abū Muḥammad Saʿd, 97
Ibn Rushd, xxxiiin, 21n
Ibn Sīnā, xxiin, xxiv, xxx, xxxii, xxxv
Ibn Sinjān, Muḥammad, xvi
Ibn Sīrīn, 39
Ibn ʿUmar, ʿAbd Allāh, 7, 96

Ibrāhīm b. Adham, 64
idolatry, 66, 70, 75, 78; see also association
Idrīs, 81
ignorance, 25, 26, 37, 71, 83; the greater sin, 25
Iḥyā' ʿulūm al-dīn, xx–xxvi; *Book of Forgiveness*, 28; *Book of Intention, Sincerity and Truthfulness*, xix; *Book of Knowledge*, xi; *Book of Ostentation*, 58; *ʿilm aḥwāl al-qalb*, xxi; main teaching, xxvi; see also al-Ghazālī, Abū Ḥāmid
ikhlāṣ, see sincerity
ilḥād, see deviation
ʿilm, see knowledge
inclination, 12, 13, 19–20, 37
insight: *baṣīr*, 44–5; limited insight, 44; people of insight, 41–2, 65
intellection (*taʿaqqul*), xxvii–xxviii
intention (*niyya*), xxvii, xxxiv; absence of, xxviii–xxix, xxxiii, xxxv, 36, 37–9, 40; Day of Resurrection, xxxii, 7, 8, 9, 31, 50; declared only 'with the tongue', xxxv, 37, 40; definition, xxxi, xxxiv, 5, 37; directionality, xxxii; examining one's intention, 35, 36; faith, xxxi, xxxv; fasting, xxvii; for every act, xxviii, 33; God's succour, xxxiv, 8; heart, 5, xxxiii, 32–3, 40; Hell, xxxii, 8, 9, 33, 34, 40, 41; Hereafter, xxxiv, 7, 32, 41, 52; inspiration from God, 40; intention is not a matter of choice, 36, 37–45; learning, xxxi, 2, 9, 88; merit of, 5–10, 16; Paradise, xxxii, 9, 40, 41; pious deeds, 28–31; prayer, xxvii, xxxi, 21, 39; pure intention, 14; purification of, xxviii, xxxii; reward according to intention, 42, 72–3; a secret only known by God, 17; sin, 24, 26, 28; sincerity, xxxvi, 1, 14, 52–3, 58, 72–3; truthfulness in, xxxvii, 85, 86, 88–9; viewpoint, 39–40; will, xxxiii, xxxv, 11; the world, xxxiv, 7, 8, 40, 52; worship, xxvii, xxviii, xxxi, xxxiii, 21; see also inclination; intention/action relationship; motive; sincerity
intention/action relationship, xxviii, 1, xxxii, xxxiv–xxxvi, 9–10, 11; 'action is through intention', 24, 26, 28, 37, 43; action without intention is useless, 21; inattentive act, 21–2; intention/act similarity, 9; intention as pillar of action, 10; 'The intention of the believer is better than his deed', xxxii, 17–23; intention without the act, 6, 7, 10, 22–3; precedence of intention over action, xxxii–xxxiii, xxxiv, 9, 16, 18; reward of intention even without the act, 6, 7; 'spirit' of action/*rūh al-ʿamal*, xxxv, 40; see also act/action
invocation, 18, 20
irāda, see will
al-ʿIrāqī, Zayn al-Dīn, xxxvii
ʿĪsā b. Kathīr, 39–40
Ismāʿīl, 81
Ismāʿīlism, xxii, xxv

Jābir b. ʿAbd Allāh al-Anṣarī, 7, 96
Jaʿfar al-Ṣādiq, 97
al-Jāḥiẓ, Abū ʿUthman ʿAmr, xxxiii
Jesus, 9, 66, 87
al-Junayd, Abū al-Qāsim, 56, 66, 84
al-Jurjānī, al-Sayyid al-Sharīf, xxiii, xxxvii, 12n, 13n, 16n

al-Juwaynī, Abū al-Maʿālī, xix

kaff, see abstaining
Kalābādhī, Abū Bakr Muḥammad b. Isḥāq, xxvi, 57n, 64n
kalām, see theology
al-Kattānī, Muḥammad b. ʿAlī, 82
al-Kharrāz, Abū Saʿīd Aḥmad b. ʿĪsā, 77–8, 92; *Kitāb al-ṣidq*, 92n
al-Khawwāṣ, Ibrāhīm b. Aḥmad, 66
killing, 8, 33
kindness, 59, 83
knowledge, 6, 25, 27, 83; *ʿālim/ʿārif* distinction, 13n; *ʿārif*, 11n–12n; *ʿilm*, 1, 11n–12n; *ʿilm/maʿrifa* distinction, 13n; knowledge/action relationship, xxv–xxvi, xxxi, xxxiii, xxxv, 1, 11–12, 13; knowledge of God, 18–19; love follows knowledge, 19; *maʿrifa*, xxv, xxviii, 11n–12n, 19; sincerity, 50, 58–9, 61; truthfulness in knowledge, 97; vain knowlegde, 28; see also learning; teaching

learning, 25–7; at the mosque, 30; intention, xxxi, 2, 9, 88; the learned, 25–7, 28n, 59, 62, 71, 87n, 88; see also disciple; teaching
love: love follows knowledge, 19; love of God, 18, 41 (sincerity, 60, 61)
lying, 50, 85–9; breaking a resolution, 91; heart, 88–9; required by the circumstances, 85–7

al-Makkī, Abū Ṭālib, xxxin, 25n, 77n; *Qūt al-qulūb*, xix, xxviii
maʿrifa, see knowledge
marriage, xxviii, 8, 33, 38
martyr, 5, 22, 75, 76, 91; types of, 91
Maʿrūf al-Karkhī, 52
al-Marwazī, Muḥammad b. Saʿīd, 56, 83
Maymūn b. Mahrān, 39–40
mendacity, 81, 82
migration, xxxi–xxxii, 75–6
mizān, see balance
modesty (*ḥayā'*), 81
monasticism, 29
morality, xxx–xxxi
Moses, 82, 97–8
mosque, 59; gaining a brother in God, 30; isolating oneself in, 29, 71; learning, 30; remembrance of God, 29–30; sojourning at, 29–30
motive (*bāʿith*), 13–16, 35, 37–8, 58, 60; four classes of, 14–16 (accompaniment, 14–15, 16, 60; assistance, 15–16, 60; association, 15, 16, 60; pure intention, 14); *ḥaraka*, 65n; motivating goal, 13; see also intention
Muʿādh b. Jabal, 32, 49, 75
Muʿāwiya b. Abī Sufyān, 50
Muʿāwiya b. Qurra, 94
al-Muḥāsibī, al-Ḥārith b. Asad, 66
Mujāhid b. Jabr, 91
Mullā Ṣadrā, xxxv
Musʿab b. Saʿd al-Madanī, 49
Musʿab b. ʿUmayr, 90–1

naẓar, see viewpoint
nearness to God, 29, 31, 33, 58; intimacy with God, 18; sincerity, 58–60
Night of the Ascension, 96
al-Nīsābūrī, Abū ʿUthmān, 65
niyya, see intention

obedience, xxviii, xxix, 40, 41, 65; truthfulness in obedience, 97; see also disobedience
Oneness (*tawḥīd*), 56, 57n, 76n, 88
ostentation, 1, 21–2, 35, 58, 78, 92–3; almsgiving, 15, 50, 53, 58, 74–7; Day of Resurrection, 58; idolatry, 75, 78; prayer, 15–16, 61, 68–70, 92–3; sincerity, 65, 66, 68–71, 73; see also sincerity, blemishes and flaws of

Paradise, 26, 41, 42n, 43, 81, 90, 95; desire for, 40, 41, 65; entering Paradise according to good deeds, 33–4; intention, xxxii, 9, 40, 41
path of God, 6, 7, 25, 44, 50, 75
perfume, 8, 31–3, 70; good intentions in the use of, 31, 32
perseverance, 19, 20
philosophy, xx, xxi–xxiii, xxix, 54n; Logic, xxii–xxiii, xxix; Neo-Platonism, xii; Peripatetic philosophy, xxii; see also *falsafa*
piety, xxvi, 10, 81; see also pious deeds
pilgrimage, xxxi, 54–5, 58, 59, 74; day of ʿArafa, 14–15, 54
pious deeds (*ṭāʿāt*), 18–20, 21, 24, 28–31, 38; absence of intention, 38–9; benefits of, 21, 22; dissimulation in, 28; intention, 28–31; perseverance in, 20; see also act/action; good deed
power (*qudra*), xxxv, 11, 12–13
prayer, xxvii, 17, 44, 60, 97; devil's deception in, 68, 70; devotional prayer, 15; intention, xxvii, xxxi, 39 (prayer without intention is void, 21); life as, xxxiii; ostentation, 15–16, 61, 68–70, 92–3; prostration, 21; *rakʿa*, 55, 71; *ṣalāt*, xxxiii, 29; sincerity, 55, 61, 69; supplications, 39; see also invocation; remembrance of God; worship
precept (*ḥukm*), 13n, 16
pride, 57n, 64n, 83
the Prophet: 'action is through intention', 24, 26, 28, 37; intention, xxxi–xxxii, 5; 'The intention of the believer is better than his deed', xxxii, 17–23; prophethood, 41n; sincerity, 66–7; truthfulness, 86, 93
prophets, 81
psyche, xxvi; *maʿrifa*, 11n; 'psychological' epistemology, 12n; psychologism, xxvi, xxvii
purification, 53; of action, 64; of intention, xxviii, xxxii; of sincerity, xxxvi, 64, 66; purifying/*ikhlās*, 57; see also sincerity
purpose (*qaṣd*), xxxiii, 11; see also intention

qaṣd, see purpose
al-Qāshānī, ʿAbd al-Razzāq, 54n
qudra, see power
Qūnawī, Ṣadr al-Dīn, xxiv, xxix, 13n
Qur'ān, x, 59; Hereafter, 41n; life, view of, xxix; *qaṣd*, xxxiii
al-Qushayrī, Abū al-Qāsim, ix, xxxvii; *al-Risāla fī ʿilm al-taṣawwuf*, xix

Ramadan, 29n
al-Ramlī, Abū ʿAbd Allāh, 81–2

Index

al-Rāzī, Abū Bakr, xxvii
al-Rāzī, Yaḥyā b. Muʿādh, 53
reason, xxvii–xxviii, 56, 83; detached from the lower senses, xxvii, xxviii
religion (*dīn*), xx, xxi, xxii, 41n, 82; bodily needs, xxviii; three pillars, 82
remembrance of God, 29–30, 41
resolve, 13, 22, 32, 35; levels of, 90; resolution is a promise, 91; truthfulness in, xxxvii, 85, 89–90; truthfulness in the fulfilment of, xxxvii, 85, 90–2
resurrection, 41n, 42n; Day of Resurrection, 8, 9, 31, 33–4, 50, 58, 91; intention, xxxii, 7, 8, 9, 31, 50; pious deeds, 33–4
riyā', see dissimulation
Ruwaym b. Aḥmad al-Baghdādī, 64

Saʿd b. Muʿādh, 90
Saʿd b. Muʿādh b. al-Nuʿmān, 96–7
sainthood (*walāya*), 97; Friend of God, 53, 97–8
sakha', see generosity
al-salaf, see forefathers
Sālim b. ʿAbd Allāh, xxxiv, 8
Sarī al-Saqaṭī, 55
scholars (*ʿulamā'*), 61–2
self-interest, 64n, 65, 72, 76, 88
servanthood, 66, 87–8; servantship to God, 40, 87–8
sexual union, xxviii, 33, 38, 41
al-Shāfiʿī, Muḥammad b. Idrīs, 32
al-Shiblī, Abū Bakr, 43, 82
al-Shikhkhīr, Muṭarrif b. ʿAbd Allāh, 53, 96
shirk, see association
shukr, see gratitude
ṣidq, see truthfulness
silence, 83, 98
sin, 9, 34, 83; aiming for the good by means of a wrong, 24–6; ignorance is the greater sin, 25; intention, 24, 26, 28; misleading through learning, 25–7; sinful acts/*maʿāṣī*, 24–8
sincerity (*ikhlāṣ*), xxvi–xxvii, 2, 49; absolute sincerity, 65; an act of self-purification, 57n; action, 55, 56; definition, 58, 60, 64, 65–7; devil, 61–3, 64n, 66, 68, 70 (delivering from devil through sincerity, 52); generosity, 50; God's countenance alone as object of search, 65; heart, 49, 57, 59, 61, 71; Hell, 50; Hereafter, 60, 61, 77n; intention, xxxvi, 1, 14, 52–3, 58, 72–3; knowledge, 50, 58–9, 61; love of God, 60, 61; merit of, 49–56; nearness to God, 58–60, 73; prayer, 55, 61, 69; the Prophet, 66–7; pure sincerity/*khāliṣ*, 57, 66, 70, 71, 74; purification of, xxxvi, 64, 66; purifying/*ikhlās*, 57, 60; rarity of, xxxvi, 55, 59, 61, 63, 76, 77; remedy of sincerity/*ʿilāj al-ikhlāṣ*, 61; a secret only known by God, 66; sincerity precludes seeing sincerity, xxxvi, 57n, 64; teaching, 59, 62; truthfulness/sincerity relationship, 2, 88–9; *al-ʿurwa al-wuthqa*, xxxvi–xxxvii; way to salvation and deliverance, 2, 55, 59; the world, 61; worship, xxvi–xxvii, xxviii, 1, 60, 61, 66–7, 71; see

also intention; motive; sincerity, blemishes and flaws of
sincerity, blemishes and flaws of, 68–78; actions mixed with ostentation or self-interest, 72–8 (judgement according to motivational power, 72–4, 76; punishment, 72; reward, 72, 74–7); association and sincerity, 57, 67, 76, 78; avoiding action for fear of fault, 77–8; discerning, 77; ostentation, 65, 66, 68–71, 73; self-interest/soul's share, 64n, 65, 72, 76, 88; vanity, 64; see also sincerity
sleep, 33, 44, 60
speech, truthfulness in, xxxvii, 83, 85–8; guarding against equivocation, 85–7; servantship to God, 87–8
stations, 92n, 94; faith, 96; fear, 92n, 94, 95, 96; truthfulness in glorification, 96; truthfulness in the stations of religion, xxxvii, 85, 94–6, 97
Stoicism, xxx–xxxi
success (*tawfīq*), 61; intention as cause of, 5
Successors (*Tābiʿūn*), 74
Sufism, ix, 9, 54n; *badal*, 54n; experience xxv, 65; *futūḥ*, 40n; Sufis' share, 65
Sufyān al-Thawrī, xxxi, 9, 34, 35–6, 39, 53, 77, 82
al-Suhrawardī, Shihāb al-Dīn Yaḥyā al-Maqtūl, xxxi
Sunna (example of the Prophet), xxxvi, 27, 70
al-Sūsī, Abū Yaʿqūb, xxxvi, 56, 57n, 64, 94
taʿaqqul, see intellection
Tābiʿūn, see Successors
Tabūk campaign, 6
taqwā, see devoutness
Ṭāʾūs b. Kaysān al-Yamānī, xxxiiin, 39, 74
tawfīq, see success
tawḥīd, see Oneness
teaching: circumstances of the seekers of knowledge, 25–7; misleading through, 25–7; sincerity, 59, 62; see also disciple; learning
theology (*kalām*), xix, xxii, xxii–xxiv, xxxv, 2n; Christian theology, xxiv; dialectical theology, xix, xxiv, xxv; *mutakallim*, xix, xxiii–xxiv, xxv, xxxiii
Torah, 9, 82–3
truthfulness (*ṣidq*), xxxvi, xxxvii, 8, 81–98; adherence to *tawḥīd*, 88; definition, 92; lack of, 56; levels of, 85, 96, 97; merit of, 81–4; perfectly truthful/*ṣiddīq*, xxxvii, 65, 81, 85, 86, 96; the Prophet, 86, 93; public/private self, 69, 70, 92–4; silence, 98; sincerity/truthfulness relationship, 2, 88–9; strive after truthfulness, 92n, 97; truthful/*ṣādiq*, 81, 85, 86; truthfulness in Divine unity, 97; truthfulness in knowledge, 97; truthfulness in obedience, 97; way to salvation and deliverance, 2; see also truthfulness, different senses of
truthfulness, different senses of, xxxvii, 85; truthfulness in action, xxxvii, 83, 85, 92–4; truthfulness in the fulfilment of resolve, xxxvii, 85, 90–2; truthfulness in intention and

will, xxxvii, 85, 86, 88–9; truthfulness in resolve, xxxvii, 85, 89–90; truthfulness in speech, xxxvii, 83, 85–8; truthfulness in the stations of religion, xxxvii, 85, 94–6, 97; see also truthfulness
al-Tustarī, Sahl, 25, 64, 83

ʿulamāʾ, see scholars
ʿUmar b. ʿAbd al-ʿAzīz, xxxiv, 8
ʿUmar b. al-Khaṭṭāb, 7, 8, 52, 62, 75, 89–90, 91, 92
Umm Salama, 7
ʿUqba b. ʿAbd al-Ghāfir, 94

vanity, 28, 61, 64
vice, 20
viewpoint (*naẓar*), 39–40

Wahb b. Munabbih al-Yamānī, 82–3
walāya, see sainthood
warfare, see fighter
wealth, 6, 58–9, 83
will, 11; action, xxxv, 11, 13; intention, xxxiii, xxxv, 11; *irāda*, 2n, 11, 68n, 85; see also intention
the world: intention, xxxiv, 7, 8, 40, 52; sincerity, 61; worldly pursuit, 76; worldly pursuit in religious activity, 75–6
worship (*ʿibāda*), xxvi–xxix, xxxi, 1; concentrated worship, 29n; existence as, xxix–xxx, xxxiii; human worship distinctiveness, xxxi; humility, 83; intention, xxvii, xxviii, xxxi, xxxiiin, 21; ostentation, 76; sincerity, xxvi–xxvii, xxviii, 1, 60, 61, 66–7, 71; supereregatory act, 27; worldly pursuit in religious activity, 75–6; see also fasting; pilgrimage; prayer

Yaʿqūb al-Makfūf, 52
Yazīd b. al-Ḥārith, 93

al-Zabīdī, Muḥammad b. Muḥammad al-Ḥusayn, xxxiii, xxxvi, xxxvii, 77n
Zachariah, 35
al-Zāhid, Abū ʿAbd al-Raḥmān, 94